SURGERY - PROCEDURES, COMPLICATIONS, AND RESULTS

SURGICAL IMPLANTS AND TISSUE PRODUCTS FOR VETERANS

OVERSIGHT ISSUES

SURGERY - PROCEDURES, COMPLICATIONS, AND RESULTS

Additional books in this series can be found on Nova's website under the Series tab.

Additional e-books in this series can be found on Nova's website under the e-book tab.

SURGERY - PROCEDURES, COMPLICATIONS, AND RESULTS

SURGICAL IMPLANTS AND TISSUE PRODUCTS FOR VETERANS

OVERSIGHT ISSUES

JERMAINE HEWITT
EDITOR

New York

For permission to use material from this book please contact us:
Telephone 631-231-7269; Fax 631-231-8175
Web Site: http://www.novapublishers.com

Additional color graphics may be available in the e-book version of this book.

Library of Congress Cataloging-in-Publication Data

ISBN: 978-1-63321-428-6

Published by Nova Science Publishers, Inc. † New York

CONTENTS

PREFACE

The Department of Veterans Affairs (VA) Veterans Health Administration (VHA) is one of the largest purchasers of surgical implants, which include biological implants, such as skin and bone grafts, and non-biological implants, such as cardiac pacemakers and artificial joints. Surgical implants fall under VHA's definition of prosthetics, which includes all items that support or replace a body part or function. Federal law grants the Secretary of VA the authority to procure prosthetics and related necessary services in such manner as the Secretary may determine to be proper, without regard to any other provision of law. This book examines factors that influence clinicians' decisions to use particular implants when multiple, similar items are available; selected VAMCs' compliance with pertinent VHA requirements for documenting open- market purchases; and VA's and VHA's oversight of VAMC compliance with implant purchasing requirements.

Chapter 1 – VHA spending on surgical implants— such as stents and bone and skin grafts—has increased to about $563 million in fiscal year 2012. Clinicians at VAMCs determine veterans' needs and request implant purchases either from a contract or from the open market (i.e., not from an existing contract). VHA requirements—which implement relevant federal regulations—include providing justifications for open-market purchases.

GAO was asked to evaluate implant purchasing by VHA. This report examines (1) factors that influence clinicians' decisions to use particular implants when multiple, similar items are available; (2) selected VAMCs' compliance with pertinent VHA requirements for documenting open- market purchases; and (3) VA's and VHA's oversight of VAMC compliance with implant purchasing requirements. GAO visited four VAMCs that serve large veteran populations and are dispersed geographically. GAO interviewed clinicians at the VAMCs, reviewed pertinent statutes, regulations, and policies and reviewed a sample of implant purchases from different vendors. These results cannot be generalized to all VAMCs but provide insights. GAO also interviewed VA and VHA officials and reviewed agency documents.

Chapter 2 – This is the Statement of Marcia Crosse, Director, Health Care, U.S. Government Accountability Office. Hearing on "VA & Human Tissue: Improvements Needed for Veterans Safety."

Chapter 3 – This is the Testimony of Philip Matkovsky, Assistant Deputy Under Secretary for Health for Administrative Operations, Veterans Health Administration, Department of Veterans Affairs. Hearing on "VA & Human Tissue: Improvements Needed for Veterans Safety."

Chapter 4 – This is the Testimony of Frank Wilton, Chief Executive Officer, American Association of Tissue Banks. Hearing on "VA & Human Tissue: Improvements Needed for Veterans Safety."

In: Surgical Implants and Tissue Products ... ISBN: 978-1-63321-428-6
Editor: Jermaine Hewitt

Chapter 1

VA Surgical Implants: Purchase Requirements Were Not Always Followed at Selected Medical Centers and Oversight Needs Improvement*

United States Government Accountability Office

Why GAO Did This Study

VHA spending on surgical implants— such as stents and bone and skin grafts—has increased to about $563 million in fiscal year 2012. Clinicians at VAMCs determine veterans' needs and request implant purchases either from a contract or from the open market (i.e., not from an existing contract). VHA requirements—which implement relevant federal regulations—include providing justifications for open-market purchases.

GAO was asked to evaluate implant purchasing by VHA. This report examines (1) factors that influence clinicians' decisions to use particular implants when multiple, similar items are available; (2) selected VAMCs' compliance with pertinent VHA requirements for documenting open- market purchases; and (3) VA's and VHA's oversight of VAMC compliance with

* This is an edited, reformatted and augmented version of a United States Government Accountability Office publication, No. GAO-14-146, dated January 2014.

implant purchasing requirements. GAO visited four VAMCs that serve large veteran populations and are dispersed geographically. GAO interviewed clinicians at the VAMCs, reviewed pertinent statutes, regulations, and policies and reviewed a sample of implant purchases from different vendors. These results cannot be generalized to all VAMCs but provide insights. GAO also interviewed VA and VHA officials and reviewed agency documents.

What GAO Recommends

GAO recommends that VA identify implants and establish a timeline to expand the volume that can be purchased from VA-negotiated contracts and improve compliance with and oversight of purchasing requirements. VA concurred with these recommendations.

What GAO Found

Clinicians at the four Department of Veterans Affairs Medical Centers (VAMC) GAO visited said that patient need and their clinical expertise were the main factors influencing their decisions of which surgical implants to use. Also, clinicians in certain specialties said they typically used one of the implants available on VA-negotiated national committed-use contracts, which generally establish a fixed price for several models of nine types of surgical implants that the Veterans Health Administration (VHA) commits to using nationally. VHA recognizes the need for expanding items covered under these contracts to fully leverage its purchasing power but, as of October 2013, had not identified additional implants to include on such contracts or established timelines for doing so. GAO also found that the availability of implants on VA-negotiated federal supply schedule (FSS) contracts rarely influenced clinicians' decisions on which implant to use. Clinicians were often not aware of the availability of surgical implants on FSS contracts, which are negotiated by one of VA's contracting offices, but for which VHA clinicians have little or no input. Clinicians told GAO that in some cases they may avoid implants on FSS contracts due to their concerns about the quality of these items.

In regard to compliance with VHA's requirements for justifying open-market purchases of surgical implants, which VHA adopted to promote adherence to relevant federal regulations, GAO found the following:

- None of the four VAMCs fully complied with requirements for obtaining waivers for open-market purchases of surgical implants because they were focusing on other priorities or lacked awareness of the requirements, among other factors.
- None of the four VAMCs fully complied with additional requirements for documenting open-market purchases that are part of a new process VHA implemented in fiscal year 2013 for surgical implant purchases over $3,000. VAMC and regional office officials attributed noncompliance mainly to insufficient VHA guidance and VA staff's inexperience in completing these requirements.
- Three of the four VAMCs did not comply with a VHA requirement pertaining to agreements with vendors that provided surgical implants to them on consignment. These agreements, which clinicians likely established to ensure timely access to implants, do not comply with a VHA requirement that consignment agreements must be authorized by a VHA contracting officer.

The Department of Veterans Affairs (VA) and VHA have begun conducting oversight of surgical implant purchases over $3,000 to assess compliance with VHA's new requirements. However, VHA officials told GAO that VA and VHA have not ensured that corrective action has been taken to address identified noncompliance because of poor communication between VA and VHA and insufficient staffing to follow up on identified issues. Furthermore, VHA assesses each VAMC's performance on metrics established for surgical implant purchasing, but it does not have a policy governing how any identified deficiencies should be addressed nor the corrective actions to be taken by VAMCs and VHA's regional networks.

ABBREVIATIONS

eCMS	Electronic Contract Management System
FAR	Federal Acquisition Regulation
FSS	Federal Supply Schedule
JOFOC	Justification for other than full and open competition
NCO	Network contracting office
NPPD	National Prosthetics Patient Database
VA	Department of Veterans Affairs
VAAR	VA Acquisition Regulation

VAMC	VA medical center
VHA	Veterans Health Administration
VITAS	Veterans Implant Tracking and Alert System

January 13, 2014

The Honorable Mike Coffman
Chairman
Subcommittee on Oversight and Investigations
Committee on Veterans' Affairs
House of Representatives

The Honorable Bill Johnson
House of Representatives

The Department of Veterans Affairs (VA) Veterans Health Administration (VHA) is one of the largest purchasers of surgical implants, which include biological implants, such as skin and bone grafts, and non-biological implants, such as cardiac pacemakers and artificial joints. Surgical implants fall under VHA's definition of prosthetics, which includes all items that support or replace a body part or function.[1] Federal law grants the Secretary of VA the authority to procure prosthetics and related necessary services in such manner as the Secretary may determine to be proper, without regard to any other provision of law.[2] VHA has exercised this authority to limit competition when purchasing prosthetics—including surgical implants— when doing so is necessary to meet veterans' clinical needs. Specifically, surgeons and other clinicians at VA medical centers (VAMC) determine veterans' needs for surgical implants. While VA has negotiated competitive contracts for a variety of surgical implants, VAMCs or VHA's regional network contracting offices (NCO) can purchase a specific surgical implant requested by a clinician from the open market with appropriate clinical justification, rather than purchasing a similar item through a competitive contract.[3] VHA's spending on surgical implants increased about 28 percent over the last four years and was about $563 million in fiscal year 2012.

At a recent congressional hearing, concerns were raised about the extent to which VAMCs and NCOs purchase surgical implants from the open market without appropriate justification, rather than purchasing such items from competitive contracts—potentially at a lower cost.[4] Concerns were also raised about VHA's oversight of VAMCs' and NCOs' purchases of surgical implants, which may have allowed insufficiently documented purchases of these items to go unnoticed. You asked us to review VHA's purchasing of surgical implants, including requirements for documenting purchases from the open market and oversight of compliance with these requirements. This report examines

1. Factors that influence clinician decisions to use particular surgical implants when multiple, similar items are available;
2. Compliance at selected VAMCs with pertinent VHA requirements for documenting surgical implant purchases from the open market; and
3. VA and VHA oversight of compliance with surgical implant purchasing requirements.

To examine the factors that influence clinician decisions to use particular surgical implants when multiple, similar items are available, we visited VAMCs in four locations: Indianapolis, Indiana; Los Angeles, California; New York, New York; and Seattle, Washington.[5] At each of the four VAMCs, we interviewed at least one clinician from each of six clinical specialties that typically use surgical implants to obtain information on the factors they consider when choosing which surgical implant to use when multiple, similar types of implants are available.[6] In total, we interviewed 28 clinicians. In addition, we interviewed staff, such as the operating room nurse manager, involved in managing surgical implants at the VAMCs.

To assess compliance at the four selected VAMCs with pertinent VHA requirements for documenting surgical implant purchases from the open market, we first identified the applicable requirements. To do so, we reviewed VA's statutory authority to acquire prosthetics—including surgical implants, applicable federal regulations—including the Federal Acquisition Regulation (FAR) and VA Acquisition Regulation (VAAR) and implementing guidance issued by VA and VHA with respect to surgical implant purchasing.[7] To learn more about VA's and VHA's surgical implant purchasing processes for surgical implant purchases from the open market, we also interviewed procurement and prosthetics officials at VA and VHA. To determine compliance with pertinent requirements, applicable to surgical implant purchases from the open market at each of the four VAMCs we visited, we reviewed documentation related to selected purchases that occurred in the first 6 months of fiscal year 2013. We reviewed the VHA data from which we selected 257 purchases. We selected these purchases to obtain a diverse group of purchases from different vendors. The purchases we reviewed represented from about 6 percent to about 83 percent of the applicable purchases at each VAMC in the first 6 months of fiscal year 2013.[8] For each of the four VAMCs we visited, we also interviewed VAMC and network officials regarding compliance with these requirements. Our findings on compliance are not generalizable beyond the purchases we reviewed. To ensure that the data we used to select purchases for review were sufficiently reliable for our purposes, we conducted a detailed data reliability assessment of the data that we used, which included checks for missing values and interviews with a VHA official knowledgeable about the data. We restricted these assessments, however, to the specific variables that were pertinent to our analyses. Our review revealed some inconsistencies and errors in the data that were attributable to data entry errors and omissions. Overall, however, we found that all of the data were sufficiently reliable for selecting our purchases for review.

To examine VA and VHA's oversight of compliance with surgical implant purchasing requirements, we obtained and analyzed VA and VHA documentation on existing or planned monitoring activities, including audit plans and reports documenting deficiencies in VAMCs' purchasing of surgical implants; interviewed VA and VHA procurement and prosthetics officials and officials from the networks that oversee the four VAMCs we visited;[9] and assessed VA and VHA's monitoring activities in the context of federal standards for internal control.[10]

We conducted this performance audit from April 2013 to January 2014 in accordance with generally accepted government auditing standards. Those standards require that we plan and perform the audit to obtain sufficient, appropriate evidence to provide a reasonable basis for our findings and conclusions based on our audit objectives. We believe that the evidence obtained provides a reasonable basis for our findings and conclusions based on our audit objectives. See appendix I for more information on our scope and methodology, including additional information on the four VAMCs we visited, the purchases we reviewed, and the steps we took to assess data reliability.

BACKGROUND

VHA provides health care services to veterans at VHA's 152 VAMCs and associated outpatient clinics. Such care can include providing surgical implants, where required—including biological implants, such as skin grafts, and non-biological implants, such as cardiac pacemakers.[11] Surgeons and other clinicians at VAMCs determine veterans' needs for surgical implants and provide VAMC prosthetics purchasing staff with documentation showing which item will be implanted in the veteran or has already been implanted in the veteran (if the surgery has been completed).

The purchasing process used by VHA varies depending on the purchase price of the implant. For purchases under the FAR's micro-purchase threshold of $3,000, prosthetics purchasing staff at VAMCs are responsible for ordering the implant that the clinician has requested for an upcoming surgery or replacing an implant in the VAMC's inventory after one has been used for a surgery, and subsequently documenting the purchase in VHA's prosthetics purchasing system.[12] This includes documenting information on the item purchased, the vendor, and the serial and lot numbers of the item implanted in the veteran. VHA has developed a new purchasing process for purchases above the FAR's micro-purchase threshold of $3,000 but below the simplified acquisition threshold of $150,000.[13] This process requires prosthetics purchasing staff at VAMCs to work with contracting officers from VHA's NCOs, with the intention of achieving greater compliance with the FAR and the VAAR.[14] VHA began implementing this process in fiscal year 2012, and VAMCs were required to implement it by the end of fiscal year 2013. As a first step under this new purchasing process, VAMC prosthetics purchasing staff begin assembling a contracting package in VHA's electronic Contract Management System (eCMS),[15] and are required to include specifications of the surgical implant requested by the clinician. Then, they submit this package to contracting officers at the corresponding NCOs who, in turn, are responsible for completing the contracting package for each purchase in eCMS. For each contracting package, NCO contracting officers have to enter over 100 data fields in eCMS. After completing the contracting package, NCO contracting officers are responsible for ordering the implant and documenting the purchase in the prosthetics purchasing system. VAMCs that had not yet implemented the new process were required to complete an abbreviated contracting package beginning in January 2013, outlined in a memorandum issued by VA's Office of Acquisition and Logistics, until they fully implemented the new purchasing process.[16] (See fig. 1 for an overview of the new surgical implant purchasing process.)

When purchasing surgical implants, VAMCs are generally required to follow a purchasing hierarchy of preferred supply sources that favor competitive contracts, as specified in the VAAR.[17] In order of preference, these competitive contracts are VA national committed-use contracts, Federal Supply Schedule (FSS) contracts, and regional or local contracts. The open market is the least preferred source, regardless of the cost of the implant. (See table 1 for a description of these types of contracts.)

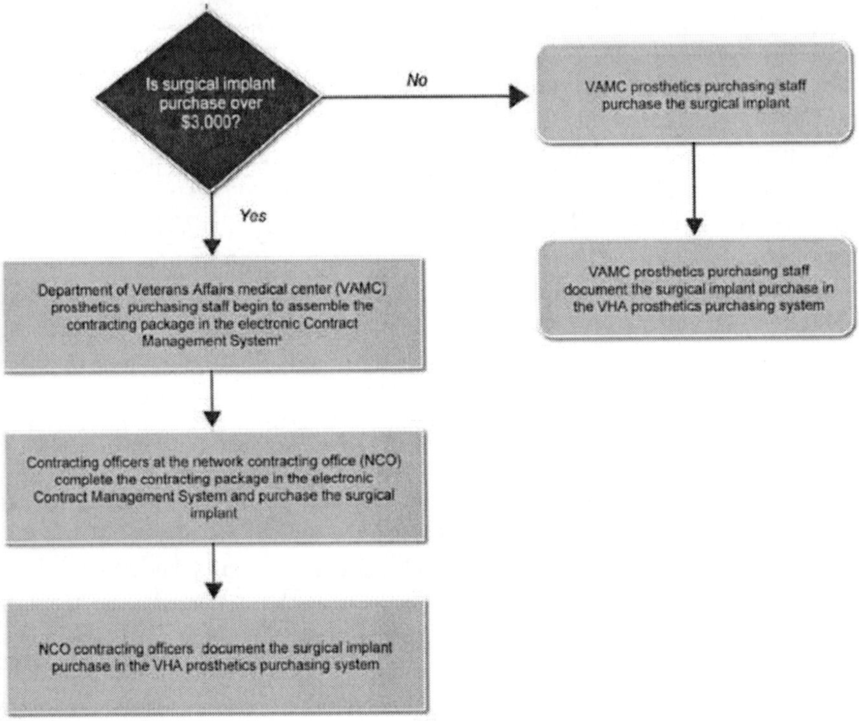

Source: GAO review of VHA documentation.

[a]As of January 9, 2013, VAMCs that had not yet implemented the new contracting process for surgical implant purchases over $3,000 were required to follow an abbreviated version of this process as outlined in a memorandum issued by VA's Office of Acquisition and Logistics. Under the abbreviated process, VAMC prosthetics purchasing staff completed an abbreviated contracting package, which they submitted to their respective NCO, and documented the surgical implant purchase in the VHA prosthetics purchasing system. VAMCs were required to fully implement the new contracting process by September 30, 2013.

Figure 1. Veterans Health Administration's (VHA) New Processes for Purchasing Surgical Implants.

Table 1. Overview of the Purchasing Hierarchy for Surgical Implants within the Veterans Health Administration (VHA)

Order of priority	Type of contract	Description
1	National committed-use contract	Negotiated by the National Acquisition Center—one of VA's contracting offices— these contracts typically establish a fixed price for several models of a certain type of surgical implant.[a]VHA commits to use the items included on these contracts throughout its healthcare system. As of September 2013, these contracts covered the following nine types of non-biological surgical implants: cardiac pacemakers and leads, implantable cardioverter-defibrillators, cardiac resynchronization treatment devices, remote monitoring devices, coronary stents, artificial hips, artificial knees, cochlear implants, and intraocular lenses. As of October 2013, these contracts only included non-biological implants.
2	Federal Supply Schedule (FSS) contract	Negotiated by the National Acquisition Center, these contracts are indefinite delivery-indefinite quantity contracts, which are awarded to multiple vendors for various types of surgical implants, both biological and non-biological. FSS contracts may include blanket purchase agreements, which allow VHA to purchase FSS items at prices that are further discounted from FSS prices, typically by agreeing to quantity requirements. Blanket purchasing agreements can be negotiated at the national, network, or VA medical center (VAMC) level.

Table 1. (Continued)

Order of priority	Type of contract	Description
3	Regional or local contract	Negotiated by VHA contracting officers, these contracts can cover a VAMC or network, and are indefinite delivery-indefinite quantity contracts. They do not cover items available on national committed-use contracts or FSS contracts.
4	Open market	Open market purchases are those that are not made through an existingcontract.

Source: GAO analysis of VAAR and VA policy document provisions.

[a]VA officials noted that these contracts are generally multiple award, indefinite delivery-indefinite quantity contracts subject to ordering procedures under FAR 16.505.

Because open market purchases are the least preferred purchasing source in VA's purchasing hierarchy, VAMCs must request a waiver to purchase on the open market instead of using a higher-priority source of supply listed in the VAAR. As further stipulated by VA policy guidance, the waiver request must show that the clinical needs of the veteran cannot be met using a surgical implant available through a higher-priority contract—that is, a national committed-use contract, FSS contract, or regional or local contract. This requirement applies regardless of the cost of the implant.

Open market purchases of surgical implants above $3,000 but below the FAR's simplified acquisition threshold of $150,000 are subject to additional documentation requirements that are part of VHA's new contracting process, which VHA implemented to foster greater consistency in the application of relevant FAR and VAAR provisions. Under this process, the contracting package for such purchases must include, among other things, a written determination of price reasonableness and, if the purchase was made noncompetitively, a justification for other than full and open competition (JOFOC) citing the rationale for the sole-source award.

Clinicians Chose Surgical Implants Based Mainly on Patient Need, Their Clinical Expertise, and, to a Lesser Extent, Implant Availability on Purchasing Contracts

Clinicians at four VAMCs cited patient need and their clinical expertise in using available surgical implants as the most important factors influencing their decisions of which surgical implants to use. In addition, certain clinicians stated that the availability of committed use contracts also influenced their decisions, whereas the availability of FSS contracts generally did not.

Clinicians Cited Their Clinical Expertise and Patient Need as the Most Important Factors Influencing Their Decision of Which Surgical Implant to Use

Many clinicians we interviewed at the four selected VAMCs stated that the specific needs of the patient were one of the two main factors that influenced their decision of which surgical implant to purchase and use. Clinicians stated that even though different types of surgical implants may appear to be identical to the lay person, there may be differences that can affect patient outcome. For example, one clinician stated that a flexible stent available through only one vendor was necessary to meet the needs of a patient with arteries that were difficult to navigate.

Many of the clinicians we interviewed stated that the other main factor influencing their decision of which surgical implant to use was their clinical expertise, which they acquired through their training and clinical experience, review of relevant literature, and interaction with vendors who supply surgical implants:

- *Training and experience*: Many clinicians we interviewed stated that their experiences in using certain types of surgical implants during their medical training and/or as a practitioner significantly impacted their decision of which item to purchase and use. For example, one clinician stated that his knowledge of different types of surgical implants, including the different features of various implants, is the result of 30 years of training and experience.

- *Review of relevant literature*: Several clinicians stated that they regularly reviewed relevant literature to help identify the surgical implants with the greatest clinical efficacy. One clinician told us that he recently switched to a different type of skin graft because a review of the literature suggested that this item was more effective than the one that he had been using.
- *Interaction with vendors*: Several clinicians told us that they work closely with vendor representatives who supply surgical implants (for example, when implanting a pacemaker, a vendor representative may be involved in testing and programming the device). Further, some clinicians with whom we spoke said that their past experience working with a particular vendor, including whether they believe that the vendor representative is knowledgeable and reliable, helps drive their decision of which implant to use. For example, a clinician stated that the reliability of vendors was important in deciding which implant to use, since some implants are not stocked at a VAMC and it is important that implants are delivered by vendors in time for scheduled surgical procedures.

Implants' Availability on Certain Purchase Contracts Influenced Clinicians' Decisions

Clinicians who performed surgical procedures for which implants were available on a national committed-use contract stated that they typically used one of the implants available on this type of contract, unless the use of these items was not appropriate, for example, for certain complex clinical indications. As of September 2013, nine types of surgical implants—cardiac pacemakers and leads, implantable cardioverterdefibrillators, cardiac resynchronization treatment devices, remote monitoring devices, coronary stents, artificial hips, artificial knees, cochlear implants, and intraocular lenses—were available through national committed-use contracts. In developing national committed-use contracts, VHA solicits input from a group of VHA clinicians to determine which items to place on national committed-use contracts and to review them for clinical efficacy.[18] Several different models of each type of implant are available on national committed-use contracts—for example, the contracts for pacemakers include models from three different vendors—thereby providing clinicians with a choice of which implant to use.

VHA has recognized the need to develop a greater number of these contracts for a variety of surgical implants, to better leverage its purchasing power and thereby pay lower prices for surgical implants. In 2011, VHA established a program management office for prosthetics to identify additional surgical implants that could be made available through these kinds of contracts and to facilitate the process of establishing and implementing them. [19] As of October 2013, an official in VHA's program executive office told us the office has been focusing on renewing and re-soliciting existing contracts that are expiring.

This official also told us that it had reviewed data on surgical implant purchases and had begun to identify items that are frequently used and high-cost. However, the official told us that it was unable to focus on developing additional national committed-use contracts because of staffing constraints, and did not have a plan or timeline for establishing new contracts. Without the establishment of national committed-use contracts for a greater number of surgical implants, VHA is not fully leveraging its purchasing power as one of the nation's largest health care systems.

While availability of implants via national committed-use contracts positively influenced their use by clinicians we interviewed, the availability of implants via FSS contracts rarely did so for a number of reasons. Clinicians at the four VAMCs we visited were often not aware of what surgical implants were available on an FSS contract, even though these contracts are preferred to open market purchases under the VAAR. For example, some of these clinicians mistakenly believed that a biological implant they were using was on an FSS contract, when in fact it was not. Clinicians at the four VAMCs we visited also lacked awareness of how to obtain information on which implants were available on an FSS contract. In addition, network prosthetics purchasing officials told us that it is difficult for both clinicians and prosthetics purchasing agents to use VHA's national database of FSS contracts to determine what specific items are available on an FSS contract. For example, the officials stated that very specific terms must be entered in the database's search field in order to obtain a useful list of items available on FSS contracts. Some clinicians stated that it would be helpful to have a user-friendly list of surgical implants available on FSS contracts, including the implant's attributes— such as its shelf life and approved clinical indication—for each surgical specialty. Clinicians at the four VAMCs we visited noted that such a list would allow them to consider FSS contract availability in making their decisions on which implant to use.

We found that one VAMC we visited had begun developing a list of skin grafts available on FSS contracts, which included their attributes—such as whether the grafts had to be stored in a freezer—to help raise awareness of items available on FSS contract.

Some clinicians at the four VAMCs we visited also stated that if there is not sufficient data to support the clinical efficacy of an implant on an FSS contract, they would not feel comfortable using it. For example, at one VAMC, a clinician noted that a specific vendor who had an implant on an FSS contract questioned why the implant was not being purchased. The clinician asked for clinical efficacy data, which—according to the clinician—was never provided, and therefore the clinician decided not to use the item. Senior VHA prosthetics and contracting officials stated that clinicians are not involved in determining which surgical implants should be available on FSS contracts, and therefore the items available on FSS contracts may not always be those that clinicians prefer to use based on their expertise and experience. Additionally, these officials expressed concern that an evaluation of the clinical efficacy of an item is not conducted in awarding FSS contracts. These officials further stated that VHA prefers to develop national committed-use contracts, for which a clinical efficacy evaluation is conducted. The director of a VHA clinical program that uses surgical implants further emphasized that clinician decisions on which implants to use should be based on proven clinical efficacy rather than inclusion on an FSS contract.

Selected VAMCs Did Not Fully Comply with VHA Requirements for Documenting Surgical Implant Purchases from the Open Market

We found that among the four VAMCs we visited: (1) none fully complied with requirements for obtaining waivers for open-market purchases of surgical implants; (2) none fully complied with additional requirements for documenting open-market purchases, which are part of VHA's new process for surgical implant purchases over $3,000; and (3) three of the four did not comply with a requirement related to consignment agreements with surgical implant vendors.

Selected VAMCs Did Not Fully Comply with VHA Requirements for Obtaining Waivers for Open-Market Purchases of Surgical Implants

None of the four VAMCs we visited fully complied with VHA requirements for obtaining waivers for open-market purchases of surgical implants. We found that one VAMC partially complied with each requirement, while the others did not comply. Current VHA requirements applicable to the four VAMCs stipulate that

- all open-market purchases of non-biological implants require a waiver approved by the VAMC Chief of Staff—regardless of the purchase price—when a comparable item would have been available through a national committed-use contract, and
- all open-market purchases of biological implants require a waiver approved by VHA's Procurement and Logistics Office—regardless of the purchase price—when a decision is made to purchase an item from the open market rather than from an FSS contract.[20]

On each of these waivers, VAMCs are required to document why the clinician chose not to use a surgical implant that is available on an existing, higher-priority contract—for example, because the clinician did not believe that the implant met a patient's need or because the clinician had concerns about the quality of the items available on contract.

Specifically, compliance with these waiver requirements was as follows at the four VAMCs we visited:

- We found that only one of the four VAMCs we visited partially complied with the waiver requirement for open-market purchases of non-biological implants, when a comparable item was available through a national committed-use contract. At this VAMC, we found that waivers were obtained for 27 of the 30 purchases we reviewed; however, 20 of the 27 waivers were incomplete, as they lacked the approving signature from the VAMC Chief of Staff. A VAMC official told us that the Chief of Staff had granted certain clinicians the authority to approve their own waivers for open-market purchases; however, VHA prosthetics officials told us that the Chief of Staff may not delegate this authority and the VAMC was unable to provide documentation to support this claim. The other three VAMCs did not comply with the requirement, meaning that they did not obtain waivers for any of the purchases we reviewed.[21] Two of these three VAMCs had a relatively high percentage of open-market purchases of non-biological implants in the first two quarters of fiscal year 2013 based on VHA data (33 percent and 35 percent, respectively) and one had a low percentage of such purchases (2 percent). Officials at two of the VAMCs told us that these waivers were not routinely obtained because they were focusing on other priorities instead, such as implementing VHA's new process for surgical implant purchases over $3,000. At the third VAMC, a prosthetics official told us that clinicians did not always fill out a waiver when asked to do so. Furthermore, because certain clinicians practice at the VAMC on a very limited basis, the official said it is difficult to ensure that they are aware of the waiver requirement and comply with it.

- We found that only one of the four VAMCs we visited partially complied with the waiver requirement for biological implants when a decision is made to purchase an item from the open market rather than from an FSS contract, whereas the other three VAMCs did not comply.[22] Officials from the three VAMCs that did not comply with the requirement told us that they did not obtain these waivers because they did not understand under what circumstances a waiver is required or were focusing on other priorities instead—such as implementing VHA's new process for surgical implant purchases over $3,000. The VAMC that partially complied with the waiver requirement for the purchases we reviewed had waivers on file, but the waivers did not include the required justification as to why a waiver was needed and did not have the required approval from VHA's Procurement and Logistics Office. Prosthetics purchasing officials at this VAMC told us that they had only recently begun to establish compliance with this waiver requirement.

Without consistent and appropriate completion of waivers for open market purchases of surgical implants, VHA lacks information regarding why surgical implants were not being purchased from higher-priority sources such as a national committed use contract or an FSS contract. This information would help VHA determine whether clinicians raised concerns about the quality or efficacy of the items available through these existing contracts, which could help VHA improve future implant purchases, and could provide a basis for holding clinicians accountable for complying with VHA requirements and procurement best practices.

Selected VAMCs Did Not Fully Comply with Additional VHA Requirements for Documenting Open-Market Purchases of Surgical Implants over $3,000

None of the four VAMCs we visited fully complied with additional requirements for documenting open-market purchases of surgical implants below the FAR's simplified acquisition threshold but over $3,000, which VHA established as part of its new purchasing process. However, all four were partially complying with the requirements. Beginning in fiscal year 2013, if a clinician requests a surgical implant over $3,000 from the open market, the following are required:[23]

- a statement affirming that the vendor's quoted price is fair and reasonable and the basis of this determination;[24] and
- a justification for other than full and open competition (JOFOC) that cites the legal authority for purchasing a surgical implant where the VAMC solicited only one source in making the open-market purchase. 25 Under VHA's new process, the JOFOC must cite one of two justifications applicable to sole-source purchases of surgical implants on the open market: (1) unusual and compelling urgency or (2) VA's special authority under 38 U.S.C. § 8123 to acquire prosthetics without regard to other provision of law.[26]

Depending on the VAMC, these documentation requirements were either completed by VAMC prosthetics purchasing staff or a contracting officer at the corresponding NCO.

Compliance with these requirements was as follows at the four VAMCs we visited:[27]

- *Fair and reasonable price determination*: The fair and reasonable price determination was not on file for between 7 and 36 percent of the applicable purchases we reviewed at three of the four VAMCs. It was on file for all applicable purchases at the fourth VAMC. However, we found that the documentation on file did not provide reasonable assurance that the price was fair and reasonable for the majority of purchases we reviewed. We found multiple instances where the documentation indicated that the determination was based on "prior experience purchasing similar items" but did not cite any prior pricing information. Not citing any prior pricing information leaves open questions about the thoroughness of the analysis conducted to determine price reasonableness. We also identified cases where the contracting officer or prosthetics purchasing agent documented the price as "fair and reasonable" when it fell within a broad range of prices. For example, a contracting officer determined that about $6,000 for a bone graft purchased from the open market was fair and reasonable because the sales prices for "similar" items was typically between $3,000 and $20,000.[28] VAMC and NCO officials we interviewed stated it is difficult to determine price reasonableness for surgical implants, in part, because they need to be knowledgeable of the exact characteristics of the item in question in order to effectively evaluate price reasonableness. They also said they believed that as contracting officers gain more experience in purchasing surgical implants, they will learn to more effectively complete this documentation. Furthermore, an NCO official stated that specific guidance from VHA on how to effectively complete the fair and reasonable price determination for surgical implants would be helpful. Ineffective market research and determination of price reasonableness may result in VHA overpaying for surgical implants.

- *JOFOC*: During our review of selected open-market surgical implant purchases over $3,000, we found two issues with respect to those purchases made on a sole-source basis for which a JOFOC was required under VHA's new purchasing process. First, the JOFOC was not on file for between 5 and 29 percent of the applicable purchases we reviewed at the four VAMCs we visited. Second, at three of the VAMCs we visited, we found that the officials responsible for completing the JOFOC selected the "unusual and compelling urgency" justification for each of the purchases we reviewed, even though some officials told us that they did not have a full understanding of which justifications applied. Specifically, we found the following:
  - Officials from two of these VAMCs told us that they were unclear about which justification to cite on the JOFOC for each purchase because they believed VHA guidance on this matter was insufficient. For example, one official responsible for completing

the JOFOC stated that he did not understand the difference between the justifications and therefore picked the one that made the most sense to him.

- Officials at another VAMC stated that they chose the "unusual and compelling urgency" justification because the contracting package for surgical implants is typically completed after the item has already been implanted and therefore this justification made the most sense to them. Furthermore, officials at this VAMC stated that a VHA draft directive on surgical implant purchasing discourages the use of VA's acquisition authority under 38 U.S.C. § 8123 to justify sole-source awards of surgical implants on the open market. Because they were discouraged from using this justification on the JOFOC, they tended to rely on the "unusual and compelling urgency" justification instead.

Moreover, while VHA requires each JOFOC to include sufficient facts and rationale to support why a specific justification was cited, only one of the four VAMCs fully provided this information for any of the purchases we reviewed. At two VAMCs, no rationale was provided for the justification selected. Furthermore, the JOFOCs at these two VAMCs were frequently missing required information, such as the contracting officer's signature, or were not completed until several months after the purchase. At the fourth VAMC, each JOFOC for the purchases we reviewed typically included a generic paragraph stating that the purchase was justified based on the determination of the clinician who requested the implant, regardless of which justification was cited. VAMC and NCO officials told us that clinicians' surgical implant purchase requests often do not contain sufficient information to support why the clinician was requesting the particular item. Because the JOFOCs we reviewed were often incomplete, VHA lacks assurance that support existed for the sole-source awards pursuant to VHA's policies at these four VAMCs.

As we discuss later, VA and VHA both identified more widespread areas of noncompliance (in the areas we describe above)—beyond the 4 VAMCs we visited—through oversight efforts they conducted at numerous VAMCs and NCOs nationwide. For example, VA's oversight identified extensive noncompliance, including inadequate fair and reasonable price determinations and missing or improperly completed JOFOCs.

VHA officials stated that they were familiar with the challenges that VAMCs and NCOs were experiencing with complying with the requirements of VHA's new process for surgical implant purchases over $3,000 and acknowledged that some of these challenges stem from a lack of sufficient guidance for implementing this new process. To address these challenges, VHA officials stated that VHA has developed additional guidance to facilitate the purchase of these items. This guidance includes (1) revised JOFOC templates to help ensure that the correct purchasing justification is cited and that an appropriate rationale is provided for using each justification and (2) additional guidance on completing the fair and reasonable price determination, which, as of November 2013, had not yet been issued. Moreover, VHA contracting officials stated that VHA plans to provide training on the documentation of purchases over $3,000; however, as of November 2013, this training had not yet been approved. In addition, VHA is developing a directive and associated standard operating procedure that outline the processes VAMCs and NCOs are expected to follow when completing contracting packages for surgical implant purchases over $3,000, including a JOFOC in the event of a sole-source purchase. As of November 2013, VHA was still in the process of providing its draft directive and standard operating procedure to stakeholders for review, and there are no established timelines for finalizing this directive and standard operating procedure, according to VHA officials. VHA officials stated that there had been disagreement between VHA prosthetics and contracting officials concerning the details of the directive and standard operating procedure–for example, which specific requirements would be the responsibility of VAMC prosthetics purchasing staff and which would be the responsibility of NCO contracting officers. According to VHA officials, these disagreements delayed the completion of these documents and disseminating them to VAMCs and NCOs.

VHA officials also told us that they are considering ways to streamline the documentation requirements for purchases over $3,000 in response to concerns from VAMCs and NCOs about the resources required to complete a contracting package for each purchase and potential delays in making purchases for surgical implants, which could result in the postponement of needed medical procedures. For example, VHA officials stated that they are considering providing VAMC prosthetics purchasing staff with ordering officer delegations, which would allow them to purchase surgical implants from national committed-use contracts, without having to work with a contracting officer to complete a contracting package for such a purchase. They told us that this would free up contracting officers' time to work on documenting open market purchases and help ensure that these purchases are appropriately documented. However, VHA officials told us that they were still in the process of evaluating the feasibility of delegating ordering authority to prosthetics purchasing staff, including addressing technical challenges with the prosthetics purchasing system, which they said currently prevent VHA from effectively implementing this change. Again, no timelines have been established to complete streamlining efforts, according to VHA officials.

Three of Four VAMCs Did Not Comply with a VHA Requirement Pertaining to Consignment Agreements with Surgical Implant Vendors

Officials at three of the four VAMCs we visited told us that the VAMCs had purchasing agreements with open-market vendors to provide surgical implants to the VAMCs on consignment, but that these agreements were not always in compliance with a VHA requirement that consignment agreements be authorized by a VHA contracting officer.[29] Under a consignment agreement, the vendor maintains vendor-owned items at the VAMC, and the VAMC purchases only the items actually used. VAMC and network officials told us that clinicians likely made these unauthorized agreements with vendors to ensure that they had timely access to the surgical implants that they preferred to use. However, they could not tell us when these agreements had been established, who had authorized them, and what the terms of the agreements were. These officials told us that the unauthorized agreements with vendors have resulted in unauthorized commitments, vendors not being paid in a timely manner, and surgical implants not being tracked in the VAMCs' inventories.[30] Furthermore, because these unauthorized agreements covered surgical implants from the open market, and the purchase prices were not negotiated, the VAMCs may have overpaid for these items.

To address these unauthorized consignment agreements, officials at each of these VAMCs or the corresponding networks stated that they were in the process of establishing authorized consignment agreements which include an agreed-upon price and quantity for each surgical implant. Having authorized consignment agreements in place may be useful in instances where the requirement for a surgical implant is immediate and it is not possible to predetermine which of several types or models are required. Establishing such agreements involves determining the types of surgical implants that clinicians need to have available on a consignment basis and obtaining a contracting officer's authorization for the VAMC to enter a consignment agreement with the vendors. At the time of our review, VHA was developing a standard operating procedure to assist VAMCs and NCOs in developing authorized consignment agreements, however, as of November 2013 they were unsure as to when it would be finalized and rolled out to the VAMCs.

VA and VHA Did Not Ensure That Corrective Actions Were Taken when Noncompliance with Surgical Implant Purchasing Requirements Was Identified

As a result of their oversight efforts, VA and VHA found noncompliance with surgical implant purchasing requirements, but did not ensure that NCOs or VAMCs took corrective action. Furthermore, VHA assesses how each VAMC is performing on key aspects of the surgical implant purchasing process, but it did not ensure that VAMCs took corrective action to address deficiencies identified or require networks to do so.

VA and VHA Found Noncompliance with Requirements for Surgical Implant Purchases over $3,000 but Neither Took Steps to Ensure that Corrective Actions Were Taken

Oversight of VAMCs' and NCOs' compliance with VHA's new process for surgical implant purchasing over $3,000 includes efforts by both VA's Office of Acquisition and Logistics and VHA's Office of Procurement and Logistics.[31] However, this oversight was not fully effective because neither VA nor VHA ensure that corrective action is taken to address noncompliance.

Recent VA and VHA oversight activities that identified significant noncompliance issues included the following:

- *VA oversight*: In February 2013, VA's Office of Acquisition and Logistics began assessing compliance with its January 9, 2013, memorandum, which required VAMCs that had not fully implemented VHA's new process for surgical implant purchasing over $3,000 to complete an abbreviated contracting package, including a fair and reasonable price determination and, if applicable, a JOFOC. This oversight effort, which examined several hundred purchases between February 2013 and August 2013, identified extensive noncompliance, including inadequate fair and reasonable price determinations and missing or improperly completed JOFOCs, which were similar to the issues we identified in our assessment.

- *VHA oversight*: In April 2013, VHA began conducting oversight of surgical implant purchases over $3,000 for the seven NCOs (and the VAMCs associated with those NCOs) that had fully implemented the new process.[32] Additional oversight is planned for fiscal year 2014 for all NCOs. An audit team from VHA's Procurement and Logistics Office is using a checklist consisting of nine questions, which assess various requirements of the purchasing process, such as whether the fair and reasonable price determination and a JOFOC, if applicable, is on file for each purchase. VHA's oversight identified noncompliance including various missing or incomplete documentation in the contracting packages for surgical implant purchases over $3,000.

While VA and VHA both conducted oversight and identified instances of noncompliance, they did not ensure that corrective action was taken. Consistent with the federal internal control standard for monitoring, which states that actions should be taken promptly in response to findings or recommendations, VA and VHA should have taken steps to ensure that noncompliance is addressed in a timely manner. 33 A senior official from VHA's Procurement and Logistics Office told us that VA's Office of Acquisition and Logistics did not provide VHA with information on the VAMCs at which noncompliance was identified, which—according to the official—would have allowed VHA to take steps to address noncompliance at the appropriate VAMCs. The official also told us that VHA's oversight is largely intended to be consultative in nature and that VHA's Procurement and Logistics Office is not sufficiently staffed to ensure that corrective action is taken.

Therefore, while VHA asked NCOs to correct areas of noncompliance, VHA did not require NCOs to document how they addressed, or plan to address, noncompliance identified in VHA oversight activities. Because neither VA nor VHA have taken steps to ensure that corrective actions are taken to address VAMC and NCO noncompliance, they lack assurance that this noncompliance is being appropriately addressed.

VHA Assesses VAMCs' Performance on Metrics Established for Surgical Implant Purchasing, but Has Not Required Networks to Ensure That VAMCs Address Deficiencies Identified

VHA assesses how each VAMC within VHA's 21 networks performs on metrics established for surgical implant purchasing, and provides the results of its assessments to the prosthetics representative at each network.[34] According to VHA prosthetics officials, VHA's assessments cover the following metrics:

- the extent to which VAMCs purchased surgical implants from a national committed-use contract or obtained a waiver allowing clinicians to use an alternative item;
- the extent to which VAMCs entered the serial number and lot number for each surgical implant purchase;
- the timeliness of each surgical implant purchase—that is, the time from which a clinician requests a surgical implant to the time the item is purchased;
- the extent to which clinicians' purchase requests for surgical implants have been fulfilled; and
- the extent to which amounts obligated for surgical implant purchases have been recorded in the prosthetics purchasing system.

Network prosthetics representatives at two of the four networks we visited told us that they regularly monitored the results from VHA's assessments and took steps to ensure that VAMCs address deficiencies VHA identified, such as correcting data entry errors. At the other two VAMCs, network prosthetics representatives did not take such steps. In both networks that did not ensure that VAMCs address deficiencies, VHA's metrics identified a relatively high rate of noncompliance with surgical implant purchases from national committed-use contracts (28 percent at one network and 13 percent at the other network in the first three quarters of fiscal year 2013). At one of these networks, this noncompliance included a high percentage of purchases missing serial numbers or lot numbers (16 percent in the first three quarters of fiscal year 2013).[35] The failure to address deficiencies uncovered through VHA's assessments may lead to higher costs for VHA and may have patient safety implications. For example, not recording the serial number or lot number for a surgical implant makes it difficult to systematically determine which veteran received an implant subject to a subsequent manufacturer or Food and Drug Administration recall.

As of November 2013, VHA did not have a policy governing how deficiencies identified through these assessments should be addressed. Accordingly, VHA officials told us that they have not required VAMCs to address deficiencies—i.e., if VAMCs do not meet an established threshold for each metric—nor did they require network prosthetics representatives to do so. Consistent with the federal internal control for monitoring, VHA or networks should establish a process to ensure that deficiencies are addressed. According to VHA officials, the directive on surgical implant purchasing that VHA is developing will require network prosthetics representatives to review each metric and ensure that deficiencies are addressed.

CONCLUSION

To its credit, VHA has established national committed-use contracts for a number of surgical implants, which can help VHA effectively leverage its purchasing power. We found that an implant's availability on this type of contract positively influenced clinicians' decisions to use that implant, but these types of contracts are only available for a limited number of surgical implants.

Establishing national committed-use contracts for a greater number of commonly used surgical implants could help reduce the number of open-market purchases of these items and ultimately reduce the costs for VA. Furthermore, steps could be taken to improve clinicians' awareness of high quality surgical implants available on FSS contracts, which may also lead to a further reduction in open-market purchases.

While VHA has requirements in place to document surgical implant purchases from the open market, selected VAMCs did not fully comply with these requirements and VA and VHA's own oversight found similar issues at other VAMCs nationwide. Greater compliance with these requirements would provide VHA with information needed to determine why VAMCs are purchasing surgical implants from the open market; it would also help provide assurance that VHA is paying a fair and reasonable price for surgical implants.

VA's and VHA's oversight of compliance with surgical implant purchasing requirements does not ensure that corrective action is taken to address identified noncompliance, which could lead to potentially serious issues remaining unaddressed.

For example, while VHA identified that at one VAMC a high number of serial numbers for surgical implants were not recorded—as required—in the prosthetics purchasing system, VHA did not ensure that this problem was addressed, resulting in potential patient safety issues remaining unresolved. Providing effective oversight of surgical implant purchasing, which includes ensuring that noncompliance is addressed, would help VA and VHA improve compliance with its applicable requirements, while potentially lowering costs for surgical implants, and improving patient safety.

RECOMMENDATIONS FOR EXECUTIVE ACTION

To expand the volume of surgical implants purchased from existing, higher-priority contracts and to improve compliance and oversight related to purchasing requirements, we recommend that the Secretary of the Department of Veterans Affairs take the following five actions:

- Create a plan that includes timelines for evaluating the benefits of developing additional national committed-use contracts for surgical implants and establishing these contracts.
- Explore options to increase clinicians' awareness of high quality surgical implants available on FSS contracts, including developing a user-friendly list for VAMC clinicians of surgical implants available on FSS contracts for each surgical specialty.
- Re-emphasize to VAMCs that waivers must be completed for open-market purchases of surgical implants, provide clear guidance to VAMCs on when and how to complete these waivers, and establish internal controls to ensure VAMCs' compliance with waiver requirements.
- Provide additional training to VAMCs and NCOs on how to properly document open-market purchases of surgical implants over $3,000, including those awarded on a sole-source basis.
- Enhance information sharing on noncompliance between VA and VHA and revise existing guidelines to require that VAMCs and NCOs document the measures they are taking to address noncompliance and report their progress (via corrective action plans) in achieving those measures through the VHA and VA management chains of command.

AGENCY COMMENTS

VA provided written comments on a draft of this report. In its comments, VA generally agreed with our conclusions, concurred with our five recommendations, and described the department's plans for implementing each of our recommendations. For example, VA will create a plan for evaluating the benefits of developing additional national committed-use contracts for surgical implants; develop and disseminate a list of surgical implants available on FSS contracts; emphasize the FSS waiver process through webinar trainings and standard operating procedures guidance; develop a checklist for proper documentation of open-market surgical implant purchases over $3,000; and require documentation of measures taken to address noncompliance identified in audits. VA also provided a technical comment, which was incorporated as appropriate.

Randall B. Williamson
Director,
Health Care

APPENDIX I: SCOPE AND METHODOLOGY

To conduct our work, we visited Department of Veterans Affairs (VA) medical centers (VAMC) in four locations: Indianapolis, Indiana; Los Angeles, California; New York, New York; and Seattle, Washington. We selected these four VAMCs because they are all classified by the Veterans Health Administration (VHA) as surgically complex facilities, serve large veteran populations and are located in different regional networks (See table 2).[1]

To examine the factors clinicians consider when choosing which surgical implant to use, when multiple, similar types of implants are available, at each of the four VAMCs, we interviewed at least one clinician from each of the following six clinical specialties that typically use surgical implants: cardiology or cardiac surgery; general surgery; orthopedic surgery; neurosurgery; podiatry; and vascular surgery. In total, we interviewed 28 clinicians. During each interview, we discussed the factors that affected clinicians' surgical implant purchase decisions and their knowledge of surgical implants available on national committed-use contracts and federal supply schedule (FSS) contracts. In addition, we interviewed staff involved in managing surgical implants at the VAMCs, such as the operating room nurse manager, surgical implant coordinator, or sterile processing service technician.

Table 2. Characteristics of VA medical centers (VAMC) Selected for Site Visits

VAMC location	Patient population served, 2011	Network number
Indianapolis, Indiana	59,372	11
Los Angeles, California	84,436	22
New York, New York[a]	75,860[a]	3
Seattle, Washington	87,483	20

Source: GAO analysis of VHA data.

[a]We visited both the Bronx and New York Harbor VAMCs. We are treating these locations as one site visit, because, due to their close proximity, certain clinical specialties are only represented at one location. We reported the total patient population for both locations. In 2011, the Bronx VAMC served 24,625 patients and the New York Harbor VAMC served 51,235 patients.

To assess compliance at the four selected VAMCs with pertinent VHA requirements for documenting surgical implant purchases from the open market, we first identified the applicable requirements. To do so, we reviewed VA's statutory authority to acquire prosthetics—including surgical implants, applicable federal regulations—including the Federal Acquisition Regulation (FAR) and VA Acquisition Regulation (VAAR) and implementing guidance issued by VA and VHA with respect to surgical implant purchasing.[2] To learn more about VA's and VHA's surgical implant purchasing processes and, in particular, surgical implant purchases from the open market, we also interviewed procurement and prosthetics officials at VA and VHA. For purposes of our review, we selected pertinent VHA requirements for documenting surgical implant purchases from the open market. We assessed compliance with these requirements at the four selected VAMCs as follows:

- To assess compliance with the requirement that a waiver be obtained and approved by the VAMC Chief of Staff for open-market purchases of non-biological implants, for which a comparable product is available on a national committed-use contract, we selected 20 purchases at one VAMC and 30 purchases at another VAMC made between October 2012 and March 2013 for which data from VHA's National Prosthetics Patient Database (NPPD) indicated that such a waiver was obtained. [3] These selected purchases represented about 35 and 80 percent, respectively, of all applicable purchases at each VAMC during this time period. We subsequently reviewed whether those waivers were, in fact, on file at the two VAMCs and whether they were complete. We selected the purchases for our review to obtain a diverse selection of purchases from different vendors.[4] At the two other VAMCs we visited, the NPPD data indicated that no waivers had been obtained, even though there were open-market purchases of non-biological implants, for which an alternative product was available on a national committed-use contract. At these two VAMCs, we interviewed VAMC and network prosthetics staff about why the waivers had not been obtained.

- To assess compliance with the requirement that a waiver be obtained when a decision is made to purchase a biological implant from the open market rather than from a Federal Supply Schedule (FSS) contract, at each VAMC, we selected 20 to 30 purchases of biological implants made between October 2012 and March 2013 which, based on NPPD data, appeared to have been purchased from the open market because the NPPD data did not indicate the purchase was associated with a contract, and assessed whether a waiver was on file for those purchases, and if so, whether the waiver was complete.[5] We selected the purchases for our review to obtain a diverse selection of purchases from different vendors.[6] We selected 110 purchases in total representing from about 9 percent to about 83 percent of all applicable purchases meeting our selection criteria at each VAMC during this time period.[7]
- To assess compliance with VHA's requirements for open-market surgical implant purchases over $3,000, including (1) a statement affirming that the vendor's quoted price is fair and reasonable and (2) a justification for other than full and open competition (JOFOC) in the case of a sole-source award, we reviewed a selection of open-market purchases over $3,000 from each VAMC to determine whether the required documentation was on file and whether it was complete. At three of the four VAMCs, which had implemented VHA's new process for surgical implant purchases over $3,000 by the beginning of fiscal year 2013, we selected 30 purchases made between October

2012 and March 2013 which, based on NPPD data, appeared to have been purchased from the open market because the NPPD data did not indicate that the purchase was associated with a contract.[8] At the fourth VAMC, we selected 15 purchases made between January 9, 2013, and March 31, 2013, which, based on NPPD data, appeared to have been purchased from the open market, because this VAMC had not yet implemented VHA's new process for surgical implant purchasing over $3,000 and therefore was not required to complete the VHA requirements until January 9, 2013. We selected the purchases for our review to obtain a diverse selection of purchases from different vendors. We selected 97 purchases in total representing from about 6 percent to about 8 percent of all applicable purchases at each VAMC during this time period.

To ensure that the NPPD data we used to select purchases for review were sufficiently reliable for our purposes, we conducted a data reliability assessment of the data that we used, which included checks for missing values and interviews with a VHA official knowledgeable about the data. We restricted these assessments, however, to the specific variables that were pertinent to our analyses. Our review revealed some inconsistencies and errors in the data that were attributable to data entry errors and omissions. Overall, however, we found that all of the data were sufficiently reliable for selecting our purchases for review. We cannot generalize our findings on compliance beyond the purchases we reviewed.

We also reviewed documentation and interviewed VAMC and network officials at the four VAMCs we visited regarding compliance with these requirements.

To examine VA and VHA's oversight of compliance with surgical implant purchasing requirements, we obtained and analyzed VA and VHA documentation on existing or planned monitoring activities, including audit plans and reports documenting deficiencies in VAMCs' purchasing of surgical implants; interviewed VA and VHA procurement and prosthetics officials; and assessed VA and VHA's monitoring activities in the context of federal standards for internal control.[9] The internal control standard for monitoring refers to an agency's ability to assure that ongoing review and supervision activities are conducted, with the scope and frequency determined by the level of risk; deficiencies are communicated to at least one higher level of management; and actions are taken in response to findings or recommendations within established timelines.

We conducted this performance audit from April 2013 to January 2014 in accordance with generally accepted government auditing standards. Those standards require that we plan and perform the audit to obtain sufficient, appropriate evidence to provide a reasonable basis for our findings and conclusions based on our audit objectives. We believe that the evidence obtained provides a reasonable basis for our findings and conclusions based on our audit objectives.

APPENDIX II: VETERANS IMPLANT TRACKING AND ALERT SYSTEM

According to Veterans Health Administration (VHA) officials, in 2008, the Department of Veterans Affairs' (VA) Office of Information Technology began developing the Veterans Implant Tracking and Alert System (VITAS), which was designed to track and retrieve identifying information—including the lot and serial number—of surgical implants placed in patients VHA-wide. VITAS was developed to address shortcomings in VHA's existing ability to track surgical implants, which may limit VHA's ability to identify and locate patients who received an implant in the event of a manufacturer or Food and Drug Administration recall. According to VHA, these shortcomings include the following:

- As we noted previously in this report, the lot number and serial number of items implanted in patients is not always entered into the prosthetics purchasing system, as required.
- While VHA clinicians from most specialties track identifying information of items implanted in their patients using standalone systems or spreadsheets that are particular to the clinicians' specialties, VA found that information on surgical implants recorded in these systems is not standardized nor is it shared across VAMCs. Furthermore, VA found that identifying information on surgical implants used in certain clinical specialties, including gastroenterology, interventional radiology, and pulmonary, is not tracked in any system.[1]

According to VA and VHA officials involved in the development of VITAS, the development of this system was suspended as of the end of fiscal year 2012 due to data-reliability and interoperability challenges. As of December 2013, VA and VHA had not decided whether to resume the development of VITAS.

End Notes

[1] VHA's definition of prosthetics includes items worn by the veteran, such as an artificial limb or hearing aid, as well as surgical implants.

[2] 38 U.S.C. § 8123.

[3] VHA negotiates national, regional, and local competitive contracts with vendors for all types of items—including surgical implants. Items that are not purchased from these contracts are referred to as open-market purchases. There are 21 NCOs throughout VHA's health care system that manage the contracting activities of the VAMCs within each of VHA's 21 Veterans Integrated Service Networks. These networks oversee the day-to-day functions of VAMCs that are within their network.

[4] *Purchasing Perspective: VA's Prosthetics Paradox, Before the Subcomm. on Oversight and Investigations of the H. Comm. on Veterans' Affairs, 112th Cong. (2012).*

[5] We selected these four VAMCs because they are all classified by VHA as surgically complex facilities, all serve large veteran populations, and are each located in a different network. VAMCs that are assigned a complex rating require special facilities, equipment, and staff for difficult operations, such as cardiac surgery. Each of the VAMCs we visited served more than 50,000 unique patients in fiscal year 2012.

[6] The six clinical specialties we selected included cardiology or cardiac surgery; general surgery; orthopedic surgery; neurosurgery; podiatry; and vascular surgery.

[7] The FAR contains government-wide regulations and establishes uniform policies and procedures used by all executive branch federal agencies for their acquisitions. VA supplements the FAR with the VAAR to establish uniform policies and procedures for all VA acquisitions. The FAR and agency supplements are codified in title 48 of the Code of Federal Regulations. With respect to VA's and VHA's implementing policies for surgical implant purchases, we reviewed, for example, VA Handbook 7408.1, *Requesting Waivers From the Requirement to Use VA Federal Supply Schedules* (June 9, 2005); and VHA Directive 2009-062, *Management of Non-Biological Implantable Devices* (Nov. 23, 2009).

[8] The range in percentages is the result of large differences in the number of open market purchases at each VAMC.

[9] Each network has a prosthetics representative who is responsible for the day-to-day management of prosthetics purchasing at each VAMC.

[10] These standards provide an overall framework for establishing and maintaining internal control and for identifying and addressing major performance and management challenges and areas at greatest risk of fraud, waste, abuse, and mismanagement. For example, under the standards for internal control, monitoring should assess the quality of performance over time and ensure that the findings of audits and other reviews are promptly resolved. See GAO, *Standards for Internal Control in the Federal Government*, GAO/AIMD-00-21.3.1 (Washington, D.C.: Nov. 1, 1999) and its supplemental guide, *Internal Control Management and Evaluation Tool*, GAO-01-1008G (Washington, D.C.: Aug. 1, 2001).

[11] Other common types of biological implants include tendons, bone chips and corneal implants, whereas other common types of non-biological implants include heart valves and stents.

[12] The prosthetics purchasing system is used to record the purchase of all prosthetics, including surgical implants.

[13] See 48 C.F.R. § 2.101 for threshold definitions and amounts. Purchases below the FAR's micro-purchase threshold of $3,000 generally require less stringent documentation than purchases above the micro-purchase threshold. The FAR also sets forth the procedures applicable to purchases below the simplified acquisition threshold at 48 C.F.R. Part 13. These procedures are designed to promote efficiency and economy in contracting and to avoid unnecessary burdens for agencies and contractors. See 41 U.S.C. § 1901(a), (c); 48 C.F.R. § 13.002.

[14] Each contracting officer works within a NCO and is overseen by managers within that office who report to VHA's Procurement and Logistics Office. VHA had previously implemented this new purchasing process for other items, such as medical supplies.

[15] eCMS is a web-based system for recording contracting actions throughout VHA.

[16] Under the abbreviated process, the prosthetics purchasing staff completed an abbreviated contracting package, which they submitted to their respective NCO, and documented the surgical implant purchase in the VHA prosthetics purchasing system.

[17] 48 C.F.R. § 808.002(a).

[18] In developing national committed-use contracts, VHA establishes teams consisting of clinicians and other subject-matter experts who are familiar with the types of surgical implants that VHA is considering including on these contracts.

[19] In 2011, VHA established a program executive office, including six program management offices. Each of the six program management offices (surgery, medical, clinical support, ancillary, advanced systems, and prosthetics) is expected to collaborate with teams of clinicians and other stakeholders, who can provide insight on identifying certain medical devices for standardization. The program management offices also coordinate with VA's contracting offices, which are responsible for establishing national committed-use contracts for standardized items.

[20] These requirements are outlined in VHA policy documents.

[21] At two of the VAMCs we visited, VHA data indicated that waivers were not being completed for open-market purchases of non-biological implants when a comparable item would have been available through a national committed-use contract. At the other two VAMCs, we selected 20 and 30 purchases for which VHA data indicated that such waivers were on file and reviewed whether those waivers were, in fact, on file and whether they were complete. At one of these VAMCs, we found that waivers were not on file, even though VHA data indicated that they were. VAMC officials told us that VAMC prosthetics purchasing staff mistakenly indicated that waivers were on file when making the purchases.

[22] The VAMC that partially complied with this requirement was different than the one that partially complied with the waiver requirement for open-market purchases of non-biological implants, when a comparable item was available through a national committed-use contract. At each VAMC, we selected 20 to 30 purchases of biological implants which, based on VHA data, appeared to have been purchased from the open market for review. For the open market purchases, we assessed whether a waiver was obtained for those purchases, and if so, whether the waiver was complete.

[23] The beginning dates for completing these requirements varied by VAMC, depending on when they implemented VHA's new process for surgical implant purchases over $3,000. We

assessed compliance against the requirements in place at each of the four VAMCs we reviewed at the time the purchases were made.

[24] The FAR provides several different methods for determining whether the vendor's price is fair and reasonable when using simplified acquisition procedures. Where possible, the contracting officer is to base price reasonableness on competitive quotations or offers. However, if only one response is received, the FAR requires a statement of price reasonableness in the contracting file, which may be based on such things as conducting market research, comparing the quoted price with the price of similar items in a related industry, or comparing the quoted price with prices found reasonable on a previous purchase, among other methods. See 48 C.F.R. § 13.106-3(a).

[25] Although simplified acquisitions are exempt from the general requirement for full and open competition, contracting officers must promote competition to the maximum extent practicable when using simplified acquisition procedures and are to include a statement in the contracting file explaining the absence of competition when only one source is solicited. See 48 C.F.R. §§ 13.104, 13.106-1(b)(1), 13.106-3(b)(3)(i).

[26] VHA's criteria for the unusual and compelling urgency exception is as follows: the surgical implant is not available for purchase on an existing contract and will be purchased on an open-market basis and (1) the delivery time does not meet the patient's medical needs and there is documentation to support the compelling special need or (2) a medical emergency exists and there is medical justification to support the need. VHA's criteria for justifying a sole-source purchase based on VA's special statutory authority under 38 U.S.C. § 8123 is as follows: the surgical implant is not available for purchase on an existing contract and will be purchased on an open-market basis because the patient's medical need cannot be met through the use of a required source of supply or service and there is medical documentation to support the need.

[27] We reviewed between 15 and 28 purchases over $3,000 at each VAMC we visited.

[28] The FAR allows the fair and reasonable price determination to be based on a comparison with similar items in a related industry.

[29] See VHA Directive 2009-062, *Management of Non-Biological Implantable Devices* (Nov. 23, 2009).Officials responsible for surgical implant purchasing at the fourth VAMC told us that they did not have any unauthorized consignment agreements in place.

[30] Unauthorized commitments refer to situations where a contract is entered into by someone other than an authorized contracting officer. We previously reported that tracking items used for patient care in VAMC inventories is important to help respond to a manufacturer or Food and Drug Administration recall of these items. See GAO, *VA Health Care: Weaknesses in Policies and Oversight Governing Medical Supplies and Equipment Pose Risks to Veterans' Safety*, GAO-11-391 (Washington, D.C.: May 3, 2011).

[31] This oversight assessed compliance with prosthetics purchases over $3,000, not just surgical implants.

[32] VHA officials told us that VHA also conducted oversight in May 2012 and June 2012 of the three NCOs that had piloted the new purchasing process.

[33] See GAO/AIMD-00-21.3.1 and GAO-01-1008G.

[34] The network prosthetic representative in each of VHA's 21 networks is responsible for supporting VHA in managing and overseeing VAMCs' prosthetics service. VHA's metrics cover all prosthetics, not just surgical implants.

[35] VA has been developing a new system—called Veterans Implant Tracking and Alert System (VITAS)—for tracking and retrieving identifying information—including the lot and serial

number—of surgical implants placed in patients. See appendix II for more information on VITAS.

End Notes for Appendix I

[1] VAMCs are categorized according to complexity level, which is determined on the basis of characteristics of the patient population, clinical services offered, and other factors.

[2] The FAR contains government-wide regulations and establishes uniform policies and procedures used by all executive branch federal agencies for their acquisitions. VA supplements the FAR with the VAAR to establish uniform policies and procedures for all VA acquisitions. The FAR and agency supplements are codified in title 48 of the Code of Federal Regulations. With respect to VA's and VHA's implementing policies for surgical implant purchases, we reviewed, for example, VA Handbook 7408.1, *Requesting Waivers From the Requirement to Use VA Federal Supply Schedules* (June 9, 2005); and VHA Directive 2009-062, *Management of Non-Biological Implantable Devices* (Nov. 23, 2009).

[3] We selected a maximum of 5 purchases per month, between October 2012 and March 2013.

[4] The NPPD is a database containing information on each surgical implant purchase that is recorded by prosthetics purchasing agents and contracting officers in each VAMC's prosthetics purchasing system. The prosthetics purchasing system allows staff to indicate whether a waiver is on file for an open-market purchase of a non-biological implant for which a comparable item is available on a national committed-use contract. We reviewed 20 and 30 non-biological implant purchases at the two VAMCs, which ranged in price from $1,496 to $22,500 and included various types of non-biological implants, such as artificial joints and cardiac pacemakers.

[5] We selected a maximum of 5 purchases per month, between October 2012 and March 2013.

[6] We identified open-market purchases in the NPPD by searching for purchases without a contract number. Prosthetics purchasing agents and contracting officers enter the contract number in the prosthetics purchasing system for any surgical implant purchase made from a contracted source. At one VAMC, only 20 purchases met our selection criteria, and we reviewed all 20 of these purchases. At the other 3 VAMCs we selected 30 purchases each. The biological implant purchases we reviewed at the four VAMCs ranged in price from $66 to $11,473 and included various types of biological implants, such as bone grafts and cornea replacements.

[7] The range in percentages is the result of large differences in the number of open market purchases of biological implants at each VAMC.

[8] We selected a maximum of 5 purchases per month, between October 2012 and March 2013. We identified open-market purchases in the NPPD data by searching for purchases without a contract number. Based on the documentation we reviewed at each VAMC, we found that some of the purchases we selected were actually made from a contracted-source, but that the contract number was not entered, and we excluded these purchases from our review. After excluding these purchases, we reviewed between 15 and 28 purchases at each of the VAMCs we visited. These purchases ranged in price from $3,019 to $20,310 and included various types of surgical implants such as stents and heart valves.

[9] These standards provide an overall framework for establishing and maintaining internal control and for identifying and addressing major performance and management challenges and areas at greatest risk of fraud, waste, abuse, and mismanagement. See GAO, *Standards for*

Internal Control in the Federal Government, GAO/AIMD-00-21.3.1 (Washington, D.C.: Nov. 1, 1999) and its supplemental guide, *Internal Control Management and Evaluation Tool*, GAO-01-1008G (Washington, D.C.: Aug. 1, 2001).

End Note for Appendix II

[1] According to VA, for these clinical specialties VHA was unable to verify that the items purchased by the prosthetics department were actually implanted in the patients for which they were purchased.

In: Surgical Implants and Tissue Products … ISBN: 978-1-63321-428-6
Editor: Jermaine Hewitt

Chapter 2

VETERANS' HEALTH CARE: OVERSIGHT OF TISSUE PRODUCT SAFETY. STATEMENT OF MARCIA CROSSE, DIRECTOR, HEALTH CARE, U.S. GOVERNMENT ACCOUNTABILITY OFFICE. HEARING ON "VA & HUMAN TISSUE: IMPROVEMENTS NEEDED FOR VETERANS SAFETY"*

WHY GAO DID THIS STUDY

In fiscal year 2013, approximately 59,000 tissue products were used to provide care to veterans at VAMCs; bone and skin grafts were the most common. While tissue products can repair the body and improve function and feeling, there is also the risk that communicable diseases can be transmitted from the donor to the recipients, potentially resulting in severe complications. FDA is responsible for regulating the manufacture of tissue products to help ensure the safety of such products marketed in the United States. For purchasing purposes, VHA considers tissue products to be a type of surgical

* This is an edited, reformatted and augmented version of testimony presented April 2, 2014 before the House Committee on Veterans Affairs, Subcommittee on Oversight and Investigations.

implant and a prosthetic—items that support or replace a body part or function.

At recent hearings of this subcommittee, concerns were raised about VA's oversight of surgical implant purchases and its ability to identify veterans who received an implant that is being recalled by the manufacturer or FDA. This testimony addresses (1) whether VHA received tissue products that may have been contaminated and (2) VHA's safeguards to prevent the receipt and use of contaminated tissues, including VHA's ability to ensure the quality of its vendors and to respond to recalls of tissue products. GAO reviewed FDA and VHA data on recalls and adverse reactions related to tissue products and VHA purchasing data. GAO also interviewed VA, VA OIG, and FDA officials on tissue product safety requirements and oversight actions. GAO focused on the policies and procedures at the VA and VHA level.

What GAO Found

Data from the Veteran's Health Administration (VHA), within the Department of Veterans Affairs (VA), do not show evidence of VHA receiving contaminated tissue products, although, it is difficult to link adverse events in recipients to such products. VA's National Center for Patient Safety (NCPS), which began operation in 1999, has not issued any patient safety alerts—mandates for action to address actual or potential threats to life or health—or advisories—guidance to address issues such as equipment design and product failure—related to tissue products potentially received by VA medical centers (VAMC) in the last 10 years. NCPS issues patient safety alerts and advisories for recalls that require specific clinical actions to ensure patient safety. Since NCPS began issuing and recording data on recalls in November 2008, NCPS has notified VAMCs of 13 recalls for tissue products from vendors from which VHA could have received affected products— none of these recalls have resulted in patient safety alerts or advisories. For 6 of the recalls, 27 VAMCs reported to NCPS that they had identified and removed the recalled products from their inventories. For the other 7 recalls, none of the VAMCs had the affected tissue products in their inventories. The 13 recalls were not issued for known tissue product contamination. Instead, most were initiated because of the possibility of contamination, such as compromise of product sterility and incomplete donor records. Further, VHA officials told us that their analysis of VHA data found no evidence of reported adverse events among VHA patients that were caused by contaminated tissue products.

According to officials from the Food and Drug Administration (FDA), post-surgical infections often occur, even in the absence of tissue use, and it is often not possible to definitively attribute such infections to a tissue product.

VHA's identification of recalled tissue products may be limited, although recent actions by the agency may help. VA and VHA rely on FDA to ensure the quality of tissue vendors—who are generally required to register with FDA—but VA and VHA policies do not require that a vendor's FDA registration status be checked for most purchases. In addition, VHA's ability to track recalled tissue products in its inventories may be limited by poor inventory management practices. After receiving a recall notice, VAMCs are required to search their inventories for recalled products; however, GAO and VA Office of Inspector General (OIG) have previously reported concerns with the completeness and accuracy of VHA's inventory data and have made recommendations to improve VHA's ability to accurately identify all recalled products in VAMCs inventories. VA is in the process of responding to these recommendations. Further, while VAMCs are responsible for checking for and accurately identifying all implanted, applied, or injected tissue products subject to a recall, GAO found that VA and VHA conduct no oversight to ensure this is done and rely on VAMCs, which may have limited ability to conduct this check. For example, VHA officials stated that it is difficult to search for information on implanted tissue products, in part, because there is no automated search capability. VA is taking steps that may enhance its ability to identify tissue products after they have been used.

VA and FDA reviewed facts GAO developed in preparing this testimony. VA and FDA provided technical comments, which were incorporated as appropriate.

Chairman Coffman, Ranking Member Kirkpatrick, and Members of the Subcommittee:

I am pleased to be here to discuss our work on the safety of tissue products used at the Veterans Health Administration (VHA), within the Department of Veterans Affairs (VA). Tissue products can be used to repair parts of the body, improve function and feeling, and restore appearance. In fiscal year 2013, approximately 59,000 tissue products were used to provide care to veterans at VA medical centers (VAMC).[1] Some of the more commonly used tissue products by VHA are bone and skin grafts.[2] Some tissue products, such as bone or tendon, may be permanently implanted into veterans in the operating room. Others, that are temporary in nature because they degrade over time or are absorbed into the body, may be applied or injected in outpatient clinics. These include skin grafts used in wound care and collagen injections.

While tissue products provide valuable methods to sustain and improve quality of life, there are also risks that they can transmit communicable disease from the donor to the recipient, potentially resulting in severe complications. [3] Transmissible pathogens can include viruses, bacteria, parasites, and fungi. The Food and Drug Administration (FDA), an agency within the Department of Health and Human Services, is responsible for regulating the manufacture of tissue products to help ensure that these products are safe and to prevent disease transmission.

VHA, which oversees all VAMCs, considers tissue products to be a type of surgical implant for purchasing purposes. [4] VHA defines these as prosthetics, which include all items that support or replace a body part or function. At recent hearings before this subcommittee, concerns were raised about VA's oversight of surgical implant purchases and the agency's ability to identify veterans who received an implant that is being recalled by the manufacturer or FDA. My remarks today will address the following two areas: (1) whether VHA received tissue products that may have been contaminated and (2) VHA's safeguards to prevent the receipt and use of contaminated tissue products, including VHA's ability to ensure the quality of its vendors and to respond to recalls of tissue products.

My remarks today are based on information we collected through reviewing agency documents and interviews with VA, VHA, and FDA officials. Specifically, to examine evidence related to possible receipt of contaminated tissue products, we reviewed VHA's analyses of purchasing data from its National Prosthetics Purchasing Database (NPPD) and NPPD data on tissue products used for treatment of veterans. We also reviewed VHA's and FDA's analyses of data on recalls and reported adverse events related to tissue products, including outcomes of these events. To determine the actions VHA takes to prevent the use of contaminated tissue products, we interviewed VA and VHA officials and reviewed documentation on VA's processes and requirements related to tissue product safety. For example, we reviewed certain aspects of VHA's oversight of and purchasing from tissue product vendors, such as whether VHA requires its vendors to have an active registration with FDA. We also reviewed VHA's tracking of, and response to, manufacturer recalls of tissue products. In addition, we interviewed officials from the VA's Office of Inspector General (OIG) regarding its related work on this topic. Our work focused on the policies and procedures at the VA and

VHA level. Our work did not focus on VAMCs, though VAMCs may have their own policies and procedures, such as those related to purchasing and responding to recalls.

To assess the reliability of the data used to prepare this statement, we gathered information from VHA and FDA on their data collection methods, including controls used to help ensure the data recorded is accurate and complete. We recently reported that NPPD data has some inconsistencies and errors that are attributable to data entry errors and omissions.[5] In our work for this statement, we also found data errors in NPPD data on VHA's tissue product vendors, such as missing or incorrect values. These errors could affect the accuracy of VHA's reports of its tissue product purchases made through contracts with vendors and purchases made on the open market.[6] However, NPPD data represent the best information available and are the data VHA relies on to determine the vendors it uses and to manage its purchasing. As a result, we found that these data were sufficiently reliable for our use in preparing this statement. We conducted this performance audit from January 2014 to April 2014 in accordance with generally accepted government auditing standards. Those standards require that we plan and perform the audit to obtain sufficient, appropriate evidence to provide a reasonable basis for our findings and conclusions based on our audit objectives. We believe that the evidence obtained provides a reasonable basis for our findings and conclusions based on our audit objectives.

We shared the information we used to prepare this statement with VA and FDA. After reviewing this information, VA and FDA provided us with technical comments, which we incorporated as appropriate.

BACKGROUND

VHA operates one of the largest health care delivery systems in the United States, providing care to more than 6 million veterans annually. Its health care system includes 151 VAMCs nationwide that offer a variety of outpatient and inpatient services, ranging from routine examinations to complex surgical procedures. VHA also provides outpatient care at more than 800 community-based outpatient clinics. Like other health care providers, VHA relies on FDA to regulate the manufacture of tissue products to help ensure the safety of such products marketed in the United States. Depending upon whether the tissue product is derived from a human tissue or an animal tissue, different FDA regulations apply.

- *Human tissue products:* FDA generally regulates human tissue products under a regulation specific to human cells, tissues, and cellular and tissue-based products.[7] Establishments that manufacture human tissue products must register annually with FDA and submit a list of each type of human tissue product manufactured.[8] FDA regulations include requirements for human tissue establishments to screen and test potential tissue donors for relevant communicable disease agents and diseases, report certain adverse events involving a communicable disease, and follow current good tissue practice requirements.[9] Some human tissue establishments may also manufacture products regulated as drugs, devices, or biological products that would be subject to additional regulatory requirements including premarket review, and the adverse event reporting requirements specific to those products.[10] FDA conducts inspections of foreign and domestic human tissue establishments to ensure they are in compliance with applicable regulations.[11]
- *Animal tissue products:* FDA generally regulates tissue products derived from animals under its medical device regulations.[12] Similar to human tissue establishments, device establishments must register annually with FDA and submit a list of each product manufactured, report certain adverse events that may have been caused or affected by use of one of its devices, and follow current good manufacturing practice requirements.[13] FDA inspects certain foreign and domestic device establishments to ensure they meet required manufacturing standards.[14] Similar to human tissue products regulated as devices, animal products regulated as devices also must meet certain premarket review requirements.[15]

VHA Data Do Not Show Evidence of Contaminated Tissue Products, Although Attributing Adverse Events to Tissue Product Contamination Is Difficult

While there have been thousands of tissue products used at VAMCs, VHA data do not show evidence of VHA receiving contaminated tissue products. However, it is difficult to attribute adverse events to tissue product contamination. VA's National Center for Patient Safety (NCPS) issues patient safety alerts, patient safety advisories, and recalls to notify VAMCs of possible receipt of unsafe or defective medical products, including tissue products. NCPS, which began operation in 1999, has not issued any patient safety alerts—mandates for action to address actual or potential threats to life or health—or advisories—guidance to address issues such as equipment design and product failure—related to tissue products in the last 10 years, according to NCPS officials.[16] NCPS issues patient safety alerts or advisories for recalls that require specific clinical actions to ensure patient safety. Since NCPS began issuing and recording data on recalls in November 2008, it has notified VAMCs of 13 recalls through September 2013 for tissue products from vendors from which VHA could have received the affected products—none of these recalls have resulted in patient safety alerts or advisories.[17] Each of these recalls could represent the recall of just one product, multiple products, or all products processed within a specific date range from a particular vendor. After NCPS issues recalls, it receives reports from VAMCs on whether recalled products were identified in their inventories—VAMCs do not report to NCPS if any products were used. Of the 13 recalls, 6 resulted in 27 VAMCs reporting back to NCPS that they had identified and removed the recalled products from their inventories. For the other 7 recalls, no VAMCs indicated that they had the affected products in their inventories. None of the 13 recalls were issued for known tissue product contamination. Instead, most were initiated because of the possibility of contamination for reasons such as compromise of product sterility, tissue recovered from donors with risk factors for communicable diseases, incomplete donor records, or manufacturers suspected to have deviated from FDA's current good manufacturing practices.[18]

Further, VHA officials told us that their analysis of VHA data found no evidence of reported adverse events among VHA patients that were caused by contaminated tissue products. Specifically, NCPS officials stated that they searched the NCPS Patient Safety Information System database, commonly known as "SPOT," which did not yield any evidence of proven adverse events being caused by tissue product contamination. SPOT contains root cause analysis reviews (investigations conducted by VAMCs to evaluate the system or process causes of reported adverse events) and patient safety incident reports (patient safety-related adverse events reported to NCPS).[19] Collectively, NCPS officials stated that their search of SPOT encompassed nearly 1 million records over more than 11 years.

Nonetheless, it is also important to note that it is difficult to determine whether adverse events are caused by contaminated tissue products. FDA officials told us that it is often not possible to definitively attribute post-surgical infections to a tissue product, despite thorough investigations of reported adverse events. FDA noted that there may be multiple possible causes of an adverse event, given the several potential sources of infection (e.g., the patient, the clinical setting, or the medical product itself). FDA also pointed out that infections following surgical procedures often occur, even in the absence of tissue use. Adverse events specifically caused by contaminated tissue appear to be rare nationwide. Of the approximately 850 reported adverse events potentially related to human tissue products received by FDA between January 1, 2006, and June 30, 2013, FDA informed us of 2 cases where infection could reasonably be attributed to the tissue product.[20]

VA Does Not Ensure Vendors are Registered with FDA; VHA's Identification of Recalled Tissue Products May Be Limited, Although Recent Actions May Help

VA relies on FDA's oversight of tissue vendors, but VA and VHA policies do not require that staff check tissue vendors' FDA registration status for most purchases. VHA's ability to track recalled tissue products may be limited by poor inventory management practices. We and VA OIG previously have reported similar concerns with VHA's inventory management practices and have made recommendations to improve VHA's ability to accurately identify all recalled products in VAMCs' inventories. Although VAMCs are responsible for checking for all implanted, applied, or injected tissue products subject to a recall, VA and VHA have no oversight to ensure this is done. VAMCs' ability to conduct this check may be limited, but VA has taken steps that may enhance its ability to identify tissue products after they have been used.

VA Relies on FDA Oversight of Tissue Vendors but Does Not Ensure Its Vendors Are Registered with FDA

The VA and VHA policies we reviewed suggest that VA and VHA do not require staff to check tissue vendors' FDA registration status for most types of purchases, despite VHA's reliance on FDA's oversight of tissue establishments to ensure the quality of the tissue products the agency receives. In addition, VA does not conduct additional oversight of its own.[21] Registration is important to ensure that tissue establishments are subject to proper federal oversight. This oversight includes, for example, FDA inspections to determine compliance with regulatory requirements pertaining to tissue product safety, such as testing and screening donors for communicable diseases. It is important to note that, according to officials, VA's vendors could include some distributors who are not required to register with FDA because they never take physical possession of tissue products. VHA has no policies requiring purchasing staff to check whether these distributors are supplying tissue products from registered tissue establishments. When discussing their purchasing requirements, VA and VHA officials told us that:

- The majority—51 percent—of tissue product purchases were open-market purchases below the Federal Acquisition Regulations (FAR) micro-purchase threshold of $3,000 in fiscal year 2013; pursuant to VHA's purchasing processes, these purchases are made by local VAMC purchasing staff.[22] VHA officials told us that the agency has no policies requiring VAMC purchasing staff to check whether tissue vendors are registered with the FDA when making these purchases.
- VHA likewise does not require VAMC purchasing staff and contracting officers to check FDA registration status of the tissue product vendor for open-market purchases over $3,000. Such purchases are rare— just 6 percent of VHA's fiscal year 2013 tissue product purchases were open-market purchases over $3,000.
- Finally, VHA can also purchase tissue products through national, regional, or local contracts, including national-committed use contracts and Federal Supply Schedule (FSS) contracts.[23] Of VHA's fiscal year 2013 tissue product purchases, 40 percent were FSS purchases below $3,000 and 2 percent were FSS purchases greater than $3,000.[24] VA officials stated that before issuing an FSS contract they check vendors' FDA registration status for medical devices and drugs, which may include some tissue products. However, there is no policy requiring staff to check a vendor's FDA registration status for other tissue products, such as those regulated under FDA's human tissue regulations. Purchases under other contracts, such as regional or local contracts are rare—less than 1 percent of purchases in fiscal year

2013—and VHA has no requirements to check a vendor's FDA registration status for these purchases.

- However, VHA officials stated that these data may undercount the number of purchases made under a contract, because NPPD does not require staff to enter contract information when recording purchases in the database. For VHA's tissue product purchases by purchase type see figure 1.

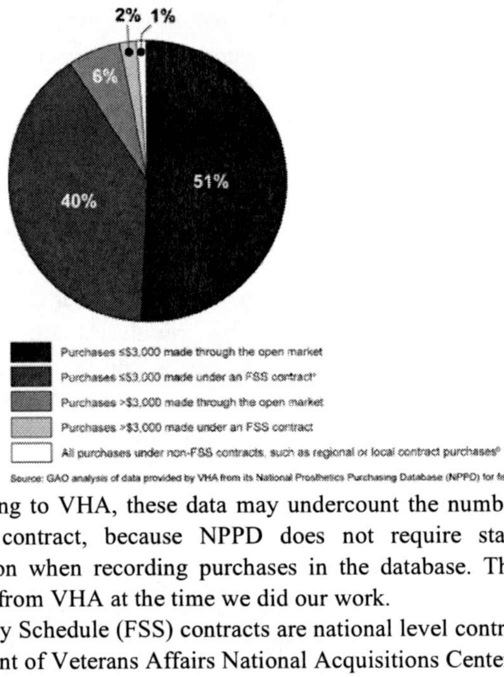

Source: GAO analysis of data provided by VHA from its National Prosthetics Purchasing Database (NPPD) for fiscal year 2013.

Note: According to VHA, these data may undercount the number of purchases made under a contract, because NPPD does not require staff to enter contract information when recording purchases in the database. This was the best data available from VHA at the time we did our work.

[a]Federal Supply Schedule (FSS) contracts are national level contracts negotiated by the Department of Veterans Affairs National Acquisitions Center.

Figure 1. Veterans Health Administration (VHA) Tissue Product Purchases in Fiscal Year 2013.

VHA's Ability to Track Recalled Tissue Products May Be Limited by Poor Inventory Management Practices

In the event of a recall, NCPS informs VAMCs, which check their inventories for the recalled items; however, in the past we and VA OIG have reported concerns with VA's inventory management practices.[25] According to VHA policy, VAMCs must have a program for responding to recalls that includes identifying numbers and locations of tissue products at the VAMCs. To ensure products are removed, VAMCs are required to report the results of these inventory searches to NCPS—which manages recalls for VHA and documents recalled products found in VAMC inventories in VHA's recall database.

However, VAMC inventory searches may be limited by poor inventory management practices. For example, in May 2011, we reported that VA may lack complete information about expendable medical supplies and reusable medical equipment in its inventories. [26] In the event of a manufacturer recall or patient safety alert for such items, VAMCs may be unable to use their inventory management systems to systematically determine whether the affected items are in their facilities. Instead, they may need to resort to a physical search, which could miss items, creating the risk that recalled products could be used in patient care. This is consistent with findings of our previous work related to VAMCs' poor inventory management practices. In our 2011 report, we recommended that VAMCs be required to enter information about all expendable medical supplies and reusable medical equipment into an appropriate inventory management system.[27] To address deficiencies we identified, VHA issued new requirements in 2011 for the management of medical supplies and equipment in VAMCs inventories. However, in 2013 we again reported that none of the VAMCs we reviewed had fully complied with all of VHA's new requirements for managing inventories, and that VAMC inventories were still incomplete. We additionally recommended that VAMCs ensure that medical supplies and equipment are tracked in the appropriate inventory management system and VA concurred with our recommendation and described specific actions that it plans to take to improve VMACs' compliance with VHA's new requirements for managing inventories, such as providing training to VAMC staff.[28] If these recommendations are effectively implemented, it will help improve VA's overall inventory management practices.

Similarly, in March 2012, VA OIG reported concerns that VHA's prosthetics inventory data—which includes tissue products—are incomplete and inaccurate.[29] VA OIG officials reported that VAMCs should use an automated inventory system—the Prosthetics Inventory Package—to manage certain prosthetic inventories including tissue products.[30] However, VA OIG told us that the few tissue products found at the VAMCs they inspected were tracked in inventory spreadsheets or logs, rather than through the Prosthetics Inventory Package. These informal tracking systems are maintained by clinical staff in the operating room and are therefore not standardized or shared across VAMCs. They are prone to error due to manual entry, thus making accurate identification of all recalled products and oversight of VAMCs' actions more challenging. In addition, when conducting the work for this statement, VA officials told us that NCPS would not notify VAMCs of recalls in certain situations; for example, if FDA reports that the recalled product is expired at the time of reporting and thus should no longer be in VHA's inventory. However, VA OIG also found that expired products often remain on VAMC's inventory shelves, which suggests that they may retain expired products that have been recalled. VA OIG recommended that VAMCs be required to conduct comprehensive physical inventories of stocked prosthetics supplies and adjust the Prosthetics Inventory Package to match inventory quantities. It also recommended that the Prosthetics Inventory Package be replaced with a comprehensive modern inventory system and a mechanism be established to identify surgical device implants stored in VAMC inventories. VA concurred with these recommendations. According to VA OIG, VA completed its physical inventory in June 2012 and plans to have a comprehensive inventory system in place in March 2015. VHA's development of a mechanism to identify surgical device implants in inventories is in process.[31]

Although NCPS tracks and responds to recalls, NCPS does not track warning letters, which notify vendors of violations found during inspections, including conditions that could lead to tissue contamination.[32] VA officials stated that they do not track warning letters because they are intended to give vendors an opportunity to take voluntary corrective action before FDA initiates an enforcement action and do not necessarily provide information on specific tissue products. For example, in 2012, FDA issued a warning letter to a vendor used by VHA that outlined problematic inspection results including conditions that could result in accidental exposure of tissue products to communicable diseases. NCPS officials explained that they did not receive this FDA warning letter, and would not expect to, as there is no recall action indicated in these letters.

Identification of Recalled Tissue Products Already Implanted, Applied, or Injected May Be Limited, but VA Is Taking Steps That May Improve Its Ability to Identify Such Products

VAMCs are responsible for checking for and accurately identifying all tissue products subject to a recall that have been implanted, applied, or injected. However, VA and VHA conduct no oversight to ensure this is done. While we did not review policies and procedures that may exist at individual VAMCs, our work suggests that VAMCs' ability to check for implanted, applied, or injected tissue products may be limited. NCPS officials told us that, unlike tissue products stored in VAMCs' inventories, NCPS is not responsible for managing and documenting recalls of tissue products that have been used and does not require VAMCs to report back the results of their search for these tissue products. Rather, according to officials, each VAMC is responsible for ensuring it tracks the recalled products to individual patients. However, there is no oversight at the VA or VHA level to make certain that VAMCs are indeed conducting this check. In addition, VHA officials stated that it is difficult to search for this information. For example, although VAMC operating room staff have been required to include the serial and model numbers of the tissue products used in the surgical patient records since 2011, VHA officials told us that there is no way to automatically search these data. Consequently, according to VHA officials, VAMCs generally rely on tissue product vendors to provide information on the medical facilities that have received recalled tissue products and staff must check individual patients' records to verify the vendor's information. Further, the quality of the data on tissue products recorded in the surgical patient records—which is entered manually by clinical staff—has not been assessed. It also does not include information on tissue products used in outpatient settings, such as skin grafts—one of VA's more commonly used tissue products. VHA's National Prosthetics Purchasing Database—NPPD—contains the serial and model number of prosthetics used for individual patients, including tissue product implants; however, VHA officials told us that NPPD is not used to track patients with implants in the case of a recall, but is generally used for purchasing and accounting purposes. Additionally, we recently reported that NPPD data was often found to be incomplete or incorrect.[33]

VA is taking steps that may enhance its ability to identify implanted, applied, or injected tissue products at VAMCs. VHA began developing a system, the Veterans Implant Tracking and Alert System (VITAS), in 2008. VITAS provides a means to track and retrieve identifying information—including the serial and lot number—of surgical implants placed in patients, including tissue products. VITAS's development was temporarily suspended due to data-reliability challenges stemming from inaccurate or missing entries in NPPD and interoperability challenges between VITAS and other VHA systems. However, VA officials told us that they plan to fund further development of VITAS in fiscal year 2014. In addition, VHA officials told us that they have established a working group to determine the feasibility of utilizing scanning and tracking technology to automatically upload tissue product implant information into electronic patient medical records.[34] Scanning a universal code on a tissue product can reduce errors in tracking implants; for example, those that occur when transcribing this information into patient records by hand. In addition, FDA issued a final rule on September 24, 2013, to establish a system to identify devices through distribution and use. The rule requires the label of medical devices to include a unique device identifier (UDI) in plain text and in a form that uses automatic identification and data capture technology, such as a bar code scanner. This rule applies to tissue products regulated under FDA's medical device regulations, and could help with the identification of these products both before and after they have been used.[35]

Chairman Coffman, Ranking Member Kirkpatrick, and Members of the Subcommittee, this completes my prepared statement. I would be pleased to respond to any questions that you may have.

End Notes

[1] For purposes of this testimony we refer to VAMCs to include the associated outpatient clinics.

[2] Other types of tissue products used by VHA include cartilage, collagen, connective tissues, heart valves, ocular tissues, and tendons. While tissue products can be derived from humans or animals, the majority of the tissue products used by VHA are derived from humans. Human tissue products that are derived from living or deceased donors are known as allografts. A patient's own tissue can also be used for a surgical reconstruction procedure—these are known as autografts. Our work did not include a review of VHA's use of autografts.

[3] Some tissues may be more prone to communicable disease than others, depending on the tissue type and processing methods used to prepare them for implantation, application, or injection.

[4] VHA codes tissue products as biological implants—a type of surgical implant—in its National Prosthetics Purchasing Database.

[5] GAO, VA Surgical Implants: Purchase Requirements Were Not Always Followed at Selected Medical Centers and Oversight Needs Improvement, GAO-14-146 (Washington, D.C.: Jan.13, 2014), 31.

[6] VA negotiates national, regional, and local competitive contracts with vendors for all types of items—including tissue products. Items that are not purchased from these contracts are referred to as open-market purchases.

[7] 21 C.F.R. pt. 1271. In this statement we refer to these regulations as FDA's "human tissue regulations." Under FDA regulations, the manufacture of human tissue includes the recovery, processing, storage, labeling, packaging, or distribution of human tissue, and the screening or testing of the tissue donor. 21 C.F.R. § 1271.3(e).

[8] 21 C.F.R. § 1271.21(a), (b). Establishments subject to these requirements include a place of business under one management, at one general physical location, that engages in the manufacture of human cells, tissues, and cellular and tissue-based products. 21 C.F.R. § 1271.3(b).

[9] Current good tissue practices are intended to ensure that tissue products do not contain communicable disease agents, are not contaminated, and do not become contaminated. They include requirements related to tissue storage and distribution, labeling, record keeping, and tracking tissue products from the donor to the consignee. 21 C.F.R. § 1271.150.

[10] 21 C.F.R. § 1271.1(b)(2).

[11] FDA conducts inspections of human tissue establishments based on available resources and uses certain risk-based priorities when determining which establishments to inspect. In fiscal years 2012 and 2013, FDA inspected 592 and 671 establishments regulated under its human tissue regulations, respectively. FDA officials stated that, due to data constraints, the agency could not determine if all establishments regulated under its human tissue regulations had an inspection. Human tissue establishments that are also regulated under FDA's drug, device, or biologics regulations are subject to inspection requirements under those provisions. 21 C.F.R. § 1271.390.

[12] 21 C.F.R. pts. 800-898. Some tissue products derived from animals may be regulated as drugs or biological products. 21 C.F.R. pts. 200-499, 600-680.

[13] A device establishment is a place of business under one management at one general physical location at which a device is manufactured, assembled, or otherwise processed. 21 C.F.R. § 807.3(c).

[14] FDA is required to inspect domestic establishments that manufacture devices that meet certain risk classifications every two years. 21 U.S.C. § 360(h). FDA is not required to inspect foreign establishments on a specific schedule.

[15] In general, unless exempt by regulation, new devices are subject to premarket review either through the premarket notification process, to determine whether a new device is substantially equivalent to another legally marketed device, or the more stringent premarket approval process, which requires the manufacturer to supply evidence providing reasonable assurance that the device is safe and effective. 21 U.S.C. §§ 360(k), 360e. On January 23, 2014, FDA issued draft guidance related specifically to medical devices containing materials derived from animal sources. FDA stated that although the use of animal derived-material in medical devices is well established, animal materials may carry a risk of transmitting communicable disease when improperly collected, stored, or manufactured. The draft guidance describes the information that should be documented at the manufacturing facility and included in any premarket submissions to FDA.

[16] Patient safety alerts or advisories are classified as such based on the severity and frequency of the incident.

[17] NCPS identified recalls related to tissue products through September 30, 2013. The products included in these 13 recalls were obtained from 11 different vendors. NCPS issues recall notifications through VHA's Alerts & Recalls intranet database to ensure that every applicable facility receives them and assigns facilities to review and take any designated actions, such as removing the product(s) from inventories. NCPS does not issue notices for all recalls. According to officials, reasons not to issue a recall notice include FDA reports that the recall is complete or terminated, the vendor reports that VHA did not receive the affected product(s), the product at the time of reporting is expired, or the product was not a remove-from-use (pull off the shelf) recall notification.

[18] One of the 13 recalls was initiated for reasons other than potential contamination.

[19] All root cause analyses are required to be reported to NCPS. According to NCPS, each VAMC can submit patient safety incident reports to NCPS using a web-based form that is standardized across VAMCs. However, officials cautioned that they rely on personnel in the field to recognize an event as a patient safety-related adverse event and enter it into the system. Since it is a voluntary reporting system, NCPS officials said they would not feel comfortable stating that every adverse event that has happened in all VAMCs is represented in the database. In addition, the level of detail in each report is often not enough to say why an event happened. Besides submitting patient safety incident reports to NCPS, each VAMC maintains its own incident reporting system, which is used by VAMC staff to report information on adverse events. Our review did not include those adverse events maintained in the individual VAMC's reporting systems.

[20] The data included those products regulated solely under FDA's human tissue regulations with the exception of cell therapy products or reproductive tissue products, which are tissue products not generally used by VHA. These data did not include tissue products that are also regulated under FDA's drug, device, or biologics regulations and are, therefore, subject to those regulations' adverse event reporting requirements.

[21] We reviewed VA and VHA-wide policies; our review did not include any policies that may exist at the VAMC-level. For example, VAMCs may have established their own VAMC-specific purchasing policies.

[22] The Federal Acquisition Regulations (FAR) are government wide regulations that establish uniform policies and procedures used by all executive branch federal agencies for their acquisitions. Purchases above $3,000 are completed through a contracting process that involves the VAMC purchasing staff and Networking Contract Office staff.

[23] These national level contracts are negotiated by VA's National Acquisitions Center. However, VHA currently has no national committed-use contracts for biologic implants, although other surgical implants could be purchased through these contracts. National committed-use contracts typically establish a fixed price for several models of a certain type of surgical implant, which VHA must use throughout its healthcare system. Federal Supply Schedule (FSS) contracts are indefinite delivery and indefinite quantity contracts awarded to vendors for various types of surgical implants and include some biologic implants, such as skin grafts.

[24] According to VA officials, there are 9 vendors with FSS contracts that could supply tissue products to VA. In January 2014, we recommended that VA develop a plan for evaluating the benefits of developing more national contracts—such as FFS contracts— with vendors of surgical implants, which could include vendors of tissue products. VA concurred with this recommendation and told us that it plans to develop a national contract procurement package for tissue products by the end of fiscal year 2014. See GAO-14-146, 26-27, 35.

[25] NCPS learns of recalls from designated officials at the regional and local level; other federal agencies, including FDA and the Department of Defense; and tissue vendors. According to VHA Directive 2008-080, vendors are required to notify VHA of any recalls or important product safety issues. VHA is required to report to NCPS any problems identified by its subordinate chain that may necessitate a recall, such as voluntary recall notices received from tissue vendors and observed clinical problems with tissue products. VHA is also required to contact NCPS should it become aware of a recall or other product safety information from vendors.

[26] GAO, VA Health Care: Weaknesses in Policies and Oversight Governing Medical Supplies and Equipment Pose Risks to Veterans' Safety, GAO-11-391 (Washington, D.C.: May 3, 2011).

[27] GAO-11-391, 19.

[28] GAO, Veterans Health Care: VHA Has Taken Steps to Address Deficiencies in Its Logistics Program, but Significant Concerns Remain, GAO-13-336 (Washington, D.C.: Apr. 17, 2013), 7-8, 25.

[29] The VA OIG report reviewed VHA's prosthetic inventory management practices. Department of Veterans Affairs, Office of the Inspector General, Office of Audits and Evaluations, Veterans Health Administration: Audit of Prosthetics Supply Inventory Management, 11-00312-127 (Washington, D.C.: Mar. 30, 2012).

[30] VA OIG 11-00312-127, 14.

[31] VA OIG, 11-00312-127, 21-22.

[32] FDA issues warning letters for violations of regulatory significance that may lead to enforcement action if not promptly and adequately corrected.

[33] We reported in January 2014 that the lot number and serial number of items used in patients is not always entered into NPPD by purchasing and procurement staff, as required. In addition, this information must be entered manually, which has the potential to cause inaccuracies in information that is entered into NPPD. GAO-14-146, 33.

[34] Officials also cited another recent change noting that as of January 24, 2014, this tissue implant data from the medical records can be captured in VHA's Corporate Data Warehouse, which would allow these data to be extracted and searched at a national level. However, access to the data is permission-based, and while VHA officials said the data could be searched at a national level, there are currently no VHA policies in place for VHA or VAMC staff to search the database during a recall.

[35] This rule does not apply to products subject only to FDA's human tissue regulations. These requirements will be phased in over a 7-year period; however, the labels and packages of implantable, life-supporting, and life-sustaining devices must bear a UDI within 2 years. 78 Fed. Reg. 58786 (Sept. 24, 2013).

In: Surgical Implants and Tissue Products … ISBN: 978-1-63321-428-6
Editor: Jermaine Hewitt

Chapter 3

TESTIMONY OF PHILIP MATKOVSKY, ASSISTANT DEPUTY UNDER SECRETARY FOR HEALTH FOR ADMINISTRATIVE OPERATIONS, VETERANS HEALTH ADMINISTRATION, DEPARTMENT OF VETERANS AFFAIRS. HEARING ON "VA & HUMAN TISSUE: IMPROVEMENTS NEEDED FOR VETERANS SAFETY"*

Mr. Chairman, Ranking Member Kirkpatrick, and members of the Committee, thank you for the opportunity to appear before you this morning to discuss the Department of Veterans Affairs' (VA) sourcing, procurement, and oversight of its biological implant purchases, including implant tissue. I am joined today by Dr. William Gunnar, National Director of Surgery, and Dr. Michael Icardi, National Director of Pathology and Laboratory Medicine Services.

* This is an edited, reformatted and augmented version of testimony presented April 2, 2014 before the House Committee on Veterans Affairs, Subcommittee on Oversight and Investigations.

BACKGROUND: INDUSTRY

Over the last 8 to 10 years, utilization of biological implants, including implant tissue, has grown significantly resulting in the doubling of value of the biomaterials market since 2004. However, the field of biological implants continues to rapidly evolve, with new advancements in tissue fabrication, nomenclature standardization, and industry governance.

ACCOMPLISHMENTS IN PROCUREMENT

On September 30, 2013, the Veterans Health Administration (VHA) successfully completed its transition of procurement duties from prosthetics purchasing agents. This transition resulted in the removal of warrants from staff who were not contracting officers. This transition also marked the final such transition for VHA – meaning that, as a rule, procurements above the micro-purchase threshold are now performed by warranted contracting officers. In the area of prosthetics alone, VHA contracting officers have conducted 38,742 procurements throughout the first quarter of fiscal year (FY) 2014. Despite our ability to effectively complete this transition, it has not come without its own challenges, and our procurement and prosthetics leadership teams convene weekly to review timeliness of procurement actions to ensure Veterans receive their needed prosthetic items, to include biological implants, on a timely basis.

DIRECTIVE REGARDING PROCUREMENT OF PROSTHETICS APPLIANCES

Title 38, Section 8123, grants broad authorities to the Secretary in the procurement of prosthetics appliances. Notwithstanding this broad authority, VHA, working with our agency's counsel, has integrated our prosthetics purchasing authority with Federal Acquisition Regulations (FAR) and VA Acquisition Regulations (VAAR) provisions. In this integration, the 8123 authority is employed as a statutory basis for a FAR Part 6 justification for other than full and open competition. What this means in practice, is that if a clinician who has been trained on a particular product has felt comfortable with that product, then she can be assured that a Government procurement official will not restrict her from selecting and using a product with which she feels competent for her patients. This application of our prosthetics authority enables our clinicians to make choices based on their medical determination of the best choice for their patients.

VHA ACKNOWLEDGES MUCH YET TO BE DONE

In complicated systems, it is always possible to improve our management and tracking controls. For more than 5 years, VHA has been able to track blood products to patient records using a barcode system, and similarly VHA Cardiology has been able to track implants to patient records. In 2011, VHA's Surgery Program implemented an implant tracking capability that also allows tracking of implants to patient records. This foundation of detailed clinical inventory management will be leveraged to provide a single comprehensive tracking mechanism that will incorporate biological implants. However, we acknowledge that we can significantly improve our tracking and inventory management of biological implantables, including tissue implants. In 2013, the Food and Drug Administration (FDA), published a final rule requiring that most medical devices distributed in the United States carry a unique device identifier, or Global Unique Device Identifier Database, and that information concerning each covered device be submitted to the global unique identification database. The rule contains staggered compliance dates. With the advent of this new identifier, systems should be able to track a specific item and associate it with the manufacturer. This tracking will enable improved adverse event tracking and will further enable greater automation in product recalls. Further, complying with FDA's Regulation of Human Cells, Tissues, and Cellular and Tissue-Based Products and Guidance for Current Good Tissue Practices, along with standards from accreditation agencies such as the American Association of Tissue Banks, Advancing Transfusion and Cellular Therapies Worldwide, and the Joint Commission, will assist in providing greater assurance over the sourcing, tracking, storage, and management of Biological implants.

WORK TEAM AND ANTICIPATED RECOMMENDATIONS

With the more recent developments in the biological implants industry and in reaction to external audits and reviews, VHA has established a work team to identify improvements to our sourcing, management and control of biological implants. This work team has been evaluating the processes currently employed by our facilities and has begun development of a proposed process to effectively manage our biological implants in a standard manner across all facilities. This work team is expected to complete its review and recommendations in the third quarter of FY 2014. We will review this team's work product and we will then begin the process of establishing a standard protocol, to include establishment of the common clinical service to manage inventory in each of our facilities.

Whether this inventory management function can be accomplished with existing technologies already deployed in VHA or with commercially available systems will be determined at the conclusion of the work team's analysis. We do, however, expect to deploy automated tracking of biological implants similar to the effective automation systems we have been using for some time now for blood bank requirements.

We have similarly charged a work team to develop a set of new, national contracts for biological implants. This work team is in the phase of procurement known as development of requirements. The work team is comprised of clinician leaders, logistics specialists, and prosthetics specialists. We fully expect our new procurement packages to establish more stringent quality standards than previous schedule contracts. We anticipate the solicitation phase of these new procurement actions to be initiated prior to the end of FY 2014.

MUST ACHIEVE BALANCE - ENABLE PHYSICIANS TO MAKE INFORMED SELECTIONS

Our core mission in VHA is the delivery of timely, quality, patient centered care. Our systems must apply controls, where appropriate, to further that core mission. We acknowledge we must continue to seek, define, and implement improvements, to our management, tracking and control of biologics items. We are committed to making the necessary changes to our policies, practices, and systems to improve. We must, however, ensure that our procurement system achieves balance and complies with all applicable Federal Laws and regulations while ensuring our physicians, whom we trust with the most critical decisions, are able to apply clinical discretion as they provide Veterans with individualized health care.

Mr. Chairman, this concludes my testimony. I appreciate the Committee's continued interest in the health and welfare of America's Veterans. At this time, I am prepared to answer your questions.

In: Surgical Implants and Tissue Products … ISBN: 978-1-63321-428-6
Editor: Jermaine Hewitt

Chapter 4

TESTIMONY OF FRANK WILTON, CHIEF EXECUTIVE OFFICER, AMERICAN ASSOCIATION OF TISSUE BANKS. HEARING ON "VA & HUMAN TISSUE: IMPROVEMENTS NEEDED FOR VETERANS SAFETY"*

Chairman Coffman, Ranking Member Kirkpatrick, and Distinguished Members of the House Committee on Veterans' Affairs Subcommittee on Oversight and Investigations:

Thank you for the additional opportunity to come before you today in support of the "Biological Implant Tracking and Veteran Safety Act of 2014." This critical legislation directs the Secretary of Veterans Affairs to adopt a standard identification system for use in the procurement of biological implants by the Department of Veterans Affairs. By building upon the success of the implementation of the Unique Device Identifier, or UDI, this legislation will ensure that biological implants used within the Department can be appropriately tracked from a human tissue donor all the way to the recipient. This critical capability for "track and trace" efforts will enhance patient safety, expedite product recalls when necessary, assist with inventory management, and improve efficiencies.

This legislation takes a bold step to expand the UDI to all tissue products. In addition to human tissue-devices (which are already covered by the UDI),

* This is an edited, reformatted and augmented version of testimony presented April 2, 2014 before the House Committee on Veterans Affairs, Subcommittee on Oversight and Investigations.

the legislation adds another product category: certain biological implants or, as termed by the Food and Drug Administration (FDA), 361 human cells, tissues, and cellular and tissue-based products, or HCT/Ps. While many of the biological implants do have company specific bar coding information, by requiring a standardized format for those bar codes, as outlined in this legislation, it will be easier for the Department of Veterans Affairs' medical facilities to utilize universal bar coding conventions and to realize the full benefit of a unique identification system. Finally, by applying a system which has been developed for devices to biological implants, such a solution should also be applicable to other health care settings and other health care systems (such as the Department of Defense health care system or the private sector).

As the Secretary of Veterans Affairs opts to adopt the standard identification protocol for tissues (both devices and non-devices), the American Association of Tissue Banks urges you to ensure that the Secretary provide a menu of options for such adoption. Under the UDI final rule, FDA has done just that by providing for multiple entities called "issuing agencies." At this time, FDA has provided for three different issuing agencies: (1) GS1, (2) Health Industry Business Communications Council (HIBCC), and (3) ICCBBA. I hope that this flexibility is maintained within the Department of Veterans Affairs. However, given that the bill language already suggests that the unique identification system is comparable to what the UDI provides, we believe the intent to provide that flexibility is inherent in the legislation.

For those of you unfamiliar with my organization, the American Association of Tissue Banks (AATB) is a professional, non-profit, scientific and educational organization. It is the only national tissue banking organization in the United States, and its membership totals *more than 125 accredited tissue banks and approximately 850 individual members*. These banks recover tissue from more than *30,000 donors* and distribute in excess of *two million allografts for more than one million tissue transplants performed annually in the U.S.* The vast majority of tissue banks that process tissue maintain AATB accreditation, and the AATB estimates that only 5-10% of the allografts distributed are from tissue donors who were not determined to be suitable by the medical director of an AATB-accredited tissue bank. The AATB does not have a similar estimation for tissue distributed by tissue distribution intermediaries.

The Association was founded in 1976 by a group of doctors and scientists who had started in 1949 our nation's first tissue bank, the United States Navy Tissue Bank. Recognizing the increasing use of human tissue for transplant, these individuals saw the need for a national organization to develop standards, promote ethics and increase donations.

Since its beginning, the AATB has been dedicated to improving and saving lives by promoting the safety, quality and availability of donated human tissue. To fulfill that mission, the *AATB publishes standards and guidance documents, accredits tissue banks, and* certifies personnel. The Association also interacts with regulatory agencies and health authorities, and conducts educational meetings.

First published in 1984 and presently in its 13th edition, the AATB's *Standards for Tissue Banking* are recognized in both the United States and around the world as the *definitive guide for tissue banking*. These Standards are the only private tissue-banking standards published in the United States, and they are the most comprehensive and detailed tissue-banking standards in the world. As such, the *AATB's Standards have served as the model for federal and state regulations as well as several international directives and standards.* Currently, the statutes and/or regulations of 19 states (i.e., California, Connecticut, District of Columbia, Florida, Georgia, Idaho, Illinois, Kentucky, Maryland, Montana, New Jersey, North Carolina, Ohio, Oklahoma, Pennsylvania, Texas, Utah, Virginia, and Wisconsin) reference AATB's Standards, institutional accreditation, or individual certification. And, these Standards are the basis of our accreditation process.

Human tissue is used in a wide variety of medical procedures in the VHA facilities, ranging from wound care management to hernia repair to orthopedic procedures. Human tissue is also used in a wide array of dental services, such as bone augmentation and gum tissue grafting procedures. In fact, according to a Government Accountability Office (GAO) report to this committee, biologics accounted for approximately $75 million in VHA acquisitions in fiscal year 2013. That same GAO report noted that one Veterans Affairs Medical Center (VAMC) had a high percentage of purchases missing serial numbers or lot numbers (16 percent in the first three quarters of fiscal year 2013).[1] I'm hopeful that this legislation will appropriately address this outstanding concern, without providing an undue burden on the health care system. For this and many other reasons, AATB supports this critical legislation.

I realize that some of you may be concerned that this legislation is duplicative and more burdensome than the FDA UDI requirements. If that were the case, it would be difficult for my organization to support its implementation. Rather, as I outlined earlier, the legislation is not duplicative of FDA's efforts because it expands the standard identification system from only devices to also cover 361 HCT/Ps. Thus, it goes beyond what Congress directed FDA to do with respect to the UDI. However, in talking to executives of the tissue banks who currently have products on the Federal Supply Schedule (FSS), all are strongly considering expanding the unique identifier to their entire product line because they acknowledge that it is an appropriate value-added benefit for hospitals and other facilities who procure tissue and, ultimately, patients, including veterans.

As for the specific timeframes outlined in the legislation, per the UDI, tissue banks will need to develop and implement the new bar coding technology for newly produced biological implants by the end of September 2015. Assuming that this legislation is enacted this Fall and that the Secretary is able to comply with the timeframes outlined in the legislation, then the timeframes for the VHA implementation and the FDA UDI implementation would coincide. Thus, by ensuring that the standard identification system conforms to the requirements and timelines outlined by the FDA, it should not place an undue burden on tissue banks; but, there will be some costs involved.

While I do not have any specific information on the implementation cost of the UDI related to tissue banks, according to a Booz-Allen Hamilton report, the primary cost of the UDI to manufacturers relates to the need to modify or replace information technology or IT systems. For manufacturers, the cost is estimated to be anywhere between $100,000 and $100,000,000, depending on the size and scale of the changes required. Given this broad range, my expectation is that, at least for tissue banks, due to their size, it's more likely that the change will be toward the lower end of the spectrum. That being said, because there is no return on investment, it is likely that tissue banks will need to increase the fee for tissue products to cover the cost of those changes.

But, such an increased cost to the VHA is worth the end result of enhancing patient safety. As the VHA has acknowledged with the previous efforts to create the Veterans Implant Tracking and Alert System or VITAS, there are current gaps in the information collection process for biological implants. As you know, VITAS was designed to track and retrieve identifying information—including the lot and serial number—of surgical implants placed in patients VHA-wide. Therefore, VITAS was developed to address shortcomings in VHA's existing ability to "track and trace" surgical implants. And, without additional developments, VHA's ability to identify and locate patients who received an implant in the event of a manufacturer or FDA recall may be limited. Unfortunately, as outlined in a recent GAO report, due to data-reliability and interoperability challenges, VITAS was suspended at the end of fiscal year 2012. And, as of December 2013, VHA had not decided whether to resume the development of VITAS. While I can understand your skepticism in requesting the VHA attempt a VITAS-like enterprise in this legislation after failing to do so before, I would note that a lot has changed since 2008 when the VHA first envisioned VITAS. First, there is now a UDI benchmark which allows those developing the necessary software for data capture to move from a design incorporating dozens of different bar coding technologies from all of the AATB-accredited tissue banks to only three different ones outlined by the three different issuing agencies. Thus, the task is much easier. In addition, the VHA is not alone in trying to develop a system for integrating the UDI-like information directly into the medical record. For instance, the Office of the National Coordinator for Health Information Technology (ONC), which is the principal federal entity charged with coordination of nationwide efforts to implement and use the most advanced health information technology and the electronic exchange of health information, is currently focused on ways in which the UDI can be better operationalized to ensure its adoption into HL7 standards – the key standards for the exchange, integration, sharing, and retrieval of electronic health information. As part of those efforts, ONC is initially focusing on implantables – the very focus of the legislation we are discussing today, suggesting that this is an area of potential "low hanging fruit" in which a small investment can reap a big reward. Therefore, the VHA will not be attempting to establish such a system alone but can partner with other governmental entities to ensure its success.

Finally, when I last discussed this legislation before the Committee, I noted my concern that the draft legislation lacked a requirement that biological implants purchased by the VHA be subject to appropriate accreditation standards. It's my understanding that those concerns are addressed in the latest version of the legislation by requiring accreditation by AATB or a similar accreditation organization. Thus, with this change, the VHA will be joining the ranks of leading medical centers of excellence which currently require all tissue to be sourced from AATB accredited tissue banks. AATB strongly supports this legislation and urges the committee to favorably report it out of committee.

I welcome your questions.

I yield back my time.

Reference

[1] http://www.gao.gov/assets/670/660105.pdf.

INDEX

D

E

F

G

H

I

Q

R

S

T

U

V

W

Y